BASKETBALL IS MY LIFE

BASKETBALL

PRENTICE-HALL, INC

IS MY LIFE

Bob Cousy
as told to Al Hirshberg

Englewood Cliffs, N. J.

LIBRARY OF CONGRESS CATALOG CARD NUMBER: 58-7019

Seventh printing........February, 1967

PRINTED IN THE UNITED STATES OF AMERICA
07246-S

Contents

CHAPTER I

The wrong side of the street

THE FIRST CANDID PICTURE EVER TAKEN OF ME SHOWS ME with an angelic look on my face, a baby shirt on my back and a big ball in my hands. It looks almost exactly like a basketball. My mother still likes to tell people in her rich French tones that it *is* a basketball and that the picture proves I was earmarked for basketball long before any of us heard of the game. She's probably right about that part, but she's wrong about the picture. I don't know what kind of a ball it is, but it's not a basketball. I didn't hold one of those in my hands until I was thirteen years old.

Although I was born and spent all of my early years on the East Side of New York, a basketball hotbed, I never saw a basketball until I moved to Long Island. The games I played when I was growing up were New York street games—stickball, boxball, stoopball—all variations of baseball. There wasn't room for anything else.

Stickball was the favorite. You can play it with only three guys. All you need is half a broomstick and a rubber ball. The baseball diamond is the street. We used to play with one

1

eye on the pitcher and the other on the corner. We never knew when a truck would come by, and we had to be on our toes. And if someone decided to park on third base, the infield had to be moved up the street.

Equipment for our street games was simple and easy to get. There were enough broken broomsticks in the neighborhood to outfit a league. And bouncing balls came a dime a dozen—or less. We got most of ours from the private tennis courts on 83rd Street across from where I lived. There was always one flying over the fence. Nobody ever came after it. They knew it was gone.

It was a typical New York neighborhood with the rich and the poor living so close together you couldn't tell the difference except for the kids' clothes. I was born in a flea-bitten tenement block on East 83rd, near the corner of East End Avenue. The place was pretty bad. We were the last to live in it. When it was condemned, we had to move out.

But across the street was an apartment block that would knock your eye out. It was a big, white brick building that stretched half a block west from the river. Next to it was the tennis club. The whole north side of 83rd Street on that block was the right side of the street. The south side, where we were, was the wrong side.

One of my earliest memories finds me sitting on our stoop watching the kids come out of the block across the street, holding on to their governesses' hands. Our older kids used to yell, "Sissy!"—and sometimes they'd get an answer.

"Go jump in the river!" a kid dressed like Little Lord Fauntleroy howled from across the street one afternoon.

"Come out of there without that lady watchdog and I'll put *you* in the river!" one of our kids yelled.

Before anyone realized what had happened, the boy had broken away from his governess and was heading across the street. The two met in the middle and started flailing away. They got in a few pretty good licks, and the boy from across the street had a bloody nose before the governess could pull them apart.

For months afterwards, the kid from our side of the street was my hero. I always figured he'd have beaten the rich boy's brains out if the governess had let him.

The moral? Well, I happen to think there's quite a point there. So much so that I've been willing to bet on a hungry kid over a well-fed kid ever since. But don't think I don't admire the rich kid for having broken away from his protector. It's just that you're more likely to win when you have to fight to live.

We got out of the 83rd Street tenement when I was about five and moved around the corner to a place on East End Avenue, which was better—it had hot running water. There were four rooms, and my mother found it a little easier to keep clean than the other place. She was forever scrubbing and scrubbing, but the odds were always against her.

All of the places in that neighborhood were practically impossible to keep clean. It was a slum world, but I was hardly aware of poverty. Loose cement, broken bricks, rotted wood, cracked windows, bulbless light sockets, smelly vestibules, ringless doorbells, knobless doors were all such a familiar part of my life that I never thought anything about them. I took bedbugs and cockroaches in stride. Today my flesh crawls at the very thought of them; but as a kid, I assumed that everyone had to put up with them. Around where I lived there was no way to keep them out except in the gleaming new apartment blocks. If anyone in the building had them, everyone had them. My mother was a fussy housekeeper, constantly working to keep the place clean, but she was fighting a losing battle. No matter how hard she worked, the bugs and the roaches always managed to get in. They came through the walls and up from the floors and down from the ceilings, and we lived with them because we couldn't do anything else.

The whole neighborhood drove my mother crazy, and the longer we lived there, the more anxious she was to get out.

"To be poor is not a sin," she used to say, "but if we must be poor, let's be poor in a clean place, free of bugs. We must go to the country, where our boy can grow up breathing fresh air."

◌

But it was years before she got her wish. And in the meantime, I was growing up as I was born—a slum kid in a slum section of New York.

I was born at 6 A.M. on August 9, 1928, on 83rd Street, but I might as well have arrived on a ship coming over here from France. My parents came to America because I was on the way. They were here only a few months when I came along. To the best of my knowledge, I was an only child, although years later, I found I had a half-sister in France, a daughter of my father's by a previous marriage.

To this day, my parents seem more like Europeans than Americans. My mother is as French as Jeanne D'Arc, although she was born in New York. Her French parents took her back to Europe when she was four years old, and she didn't return here until she was over thirty. She spent most of her life in Dijon, in the heart of a French wine-growing belt close to the German border.

She never learned to speak English until she came over here with my father just before I was born. She was raised as a French girl, and she still speaks only French at home. Everything about her is French. Her maiden name was Juliet

Corlet, which is about as French as you can get. She is a tall, angular woman who once was very beautiful. Her deep brown eyes are the most expressive I have ever seen. She can carry on a conversation with them. She is excitable and nervous and fast-moving. The slightest change affects her personality. She can be deep in the doldrums one minute and up in the clouds the next.

Her teachers were Catholic nuns, and some of the best friends she has ever had, both here and abroad, were nuns. After she grew up, she worked in Paris and Dijon, sometimes as a secretary and sometimes as a teacher of French. She had some Austrian pupils, who drifted across the border after the end of the first World War.

My father came over from Alsace-Lorraine. He was a farmer for many years, but he began driving a taxicab while he was still over there. He was a cab driver from almost the moment he arrived here. He drove a hack in New York for twenty-five years before retiring when it finally became too much for him. He is now a maintenance man at Idlewild International Airport, not far from his home in St. Albans, Long Island.

He's quite different from my mother in almost all respects. She is tall and thin; he is short and stocky. She carries her emotions in her face; he hides his behind a calm exterior. She gets excited easily; nothing seems to bother my father. He is a plodder, a patient, hard-working man who figures that everything will come to him who waits; my mother has no patience whatever. When there is something to be done, she wants it done on the spot. She's always in a hurry; my father never is.

I inherited my own outward calm from my father. I also got an intensity of purpose from him, though my mother has that too. Both my parents have always set goals for themselves and then reached for them—only their methods of getting there were different. I've been setting goals for myself all my life. I got my nervous energy from my mother, and I also inherited her tall, thin frame and her hands and feet, which are unusually large. From my father I inherited my poker face and ability to accept things as they happen.

Once when I was a kid, somebody hit me in the head with a rock. I came home screaming, an impressively gory sight. My mother nearly fainted when she saw me. She gathered me up in her arms and yelled, "What shall we do? What shall we do?"

My father looked at the cut, then calmly remarked, "Put a little ice on and forget it. He'll be all right."

She did, and I was.

My grandmother—my mother's mother—also lived with us and from time to time my uncle, Charles Roth, paid us a visit. He was a jolly, friendly guy who knew America better than anyone in the household. He had worked here for years, first as a waiter and later as a *maître d'hôtel*. Years later, I discovered that he had once been *maître de* of the Hotel Touraine in Boston.

My grandmother was a very good Catholic, and she was determined that I should be one.

"There is no substitute for the Church," she used to tell me. "You must go regularly and do what the priest tells you."

She didn't stop with just telling me to go. She took me every Sunday and made sure that I went to a parochial school while we were living in Manhattan. My father often worked on Sundays, and my mother was often so busy fighting the battle of the bugs that Sunday morning sometimes wasn't long enough for church. But my grandmother never missed.

I talked nothing but French the first five years of my life. I must have been a queer little bird at that, sticking close to my mother or my grandmother, talking a strange language whenever I went out in the street and looking like a dope whenever anyone talked to me. Actually, I didn't pick up a single word of English until I started school.

I was five years old when I went to kindergarten for the first time. My grandmother took me to St. Katherine's parochial school, near the corner of East 86th Street and Third Avenue. The school was free to those who couldn't afford to pay tuition, and, of course, that included us. I went to St. Katherine's all during my East Side days.

At first, the other kids and I couldn't figure each other out. I understood a little of what they were saying, but they understood practically nothing I said. But I don't think this situation lasted long. I picked up English fast enough so that I could speak it pretty well before the year was over.

To this day, I have Gallic speech characteristics that belong to my very young childhood. I roll my r's, a throwback to the old days. It's very desirable for opera singers, I'm told, but it doesn't do much for an American basketball player.

Aside from my French accent, I've always had a slight speech impediment that caused me to lisp. Maybe I roll my r's today because I couldn't pronounce them at all when I was a kid. I made l's out of r's for years, and when I'm very tired, I still do.

Howie McHugh, the publicity director of the Boston Celtics, loves to burlesque my explanation of how I scored a last-second winning basket one night. According to McHugh, I said, "I dlibbled a riddle and dlibbled a riddle and rooked at the crock and dlibbled a riddle more and then I sank a light-hander." (English translation: "I dribbled a little and dribbled a little and looked at the clock and dribbled a little more and then I sank a right-hander.")

The only trouble with Howie's version, which fractures me

when he pulls it, is that while I have trouble with r's, I don't have any with l's—they're just all l's.

Once, while I was still living on the East Side, a speech teacher made me repeat this sentence: "Around the rugged rock, the ragged rascal ran."

For years it came out "Alound the lugged lock, the lagged lascal lan." And sometimes it still does.

The kids around where I lived started calling me Frenchy, but it eventually developed into Flenchy. I was Flenchy right up to the time we moved away. I suppose if I ever ran into one of the guys who knew me as a youngster, he'd still call me Flenchy.

After we moved around the corner from 83rd to East End Avenue, I still played on 83rd Street, but my mother could see me from the window of our tenement. She couldn't yell loud enough for me to hear so she used to wave a handkerchief whenever she wanted me. Sooner or later, one of the kids would see it and yell, "Hey, Flenchy, the handkerchief's out," and I'd run home. And as I ran, I could hear a chorus as the other kids joined in with "Hey, Flenchy, the handkerchief's out."

I didn't mind—in fact, I think I sort of liked it. The kids weren't malicious. They just got a kick out of it. They always smiled when they said it, and so did I.

But once I started speaking English, I wanted to stop speaking French, and I guess I resented having to speak it at home. I was like an immigrant kid. I wanted to be an American through and through, and I wanted to talk like an American. But I never told my folks how I felt. I just wished they spoke English at home.

For years I did all my thinking in French, and when I had nightmares, I talked French in my sleep. I still do occasionally. I don't think it's a subconscious affinity for my childhood tongue because even now I don't speak French unless I have to. But it wasn't until I reached high school age that I really began thinking in English.

On the East Side, the Cousys were among what the social service workers call the underprivileged, but I didn't feel very underprivileged. I had a whale of a good time out of life, playing stickball and stoopball and boxball and releav-O and roasting mickeys in tin cans and swimming raw among the coal and garbage barges on the East River and hooking rides on trucks and coasting in traffic in winter and swiping bananas off pushcarts and collecting everything from string and nails to match covers and bottle caps.

Once another kid and I had a race to see who could collect the most valve caps from automobile tires. There was only one place to get them—off automobiles. We used to go along the street, unscrewing one after another, shoving them in our pockets and sneaking them upstairs to add to our collections.

I was doing pretty well until I got careless one day. I was so busy taking caps off tire valves that I didn't notice what was going on around me. I nearly jumped out of my skin when a guy grabbed me by the shoulder and yelled, "What's the big idea?"

He jerked me around, and I looked up into the face that must have been used as a model for pictures of the giant in "Jack and the Beanstalk." I was only eight or nine, and the man seemed about nine feet tall. He needed a shave, and his breath smelled and his black eyes bored into me. If I spoke French during nightmares, this was the guy I was talking to.

I was too scared to answer.

"Put those back!"

The guy, still keeping hold of me, lowered me far enough so that I could screw the valve cap back. Then he walked me

around the car while I put the rest back. And when I'd finished doing that, he said, "How many more of those have you
got?"

"A whole collection," I managed to stammer.

"Where?"

"Home."

"Where do you live?"

I jerked my thumb towards East End Avenue.

"Well, go up and bring them down."

He let go of me, and I ran. And when I reached our building, I dashed upstairs, ignored my mother's questions,
grabbed the bag of valve caps and rushed back down. When
I got back to where this guy was standing, he was talking to
a cop, and a crowd was gathering. I heard somebody whisper,
"Flenchy's in trouble," and I had visions of the guillotine.

"Empty that bag," the guy yelled, "and show this cop what
a lousy little thief you are!"

So while the man kept yelling and the cop glared and the
crowd cluck-clucked, I turned the bag upside down and
watched weepily while my precious valve caps rolled in the
gutter. Pretty soon my mother, frightened to death and weep-
ing herself, came down and started talking to the cop. I don't
know what they said to each other, but after a while my
mother said in French, "Come on, Roby," and I meekly followed her home. That was the end of the contest. The other
kid retired with the undisputed valve cap collecting championship of the neighborhood.

I might have been having a good time, but nobody else in
the family was. My father often worked seven days a week
trying to make enough money from the hack to put something aside for the future. He was just as anxious as my
mother to get away from the East Side, but he was having a
tough climb. It was right in the middle of the depression, and

people weren't taking cabs if they could walk or take a subway.

I used to hear my mother tell him, "We've got to get Roby out into the country." He'd nod his head, then drive off in his cab.

When my father wasn't working on Sundays, he'd sometimes take us for a ride in the country. The first memory I have of one of those rides was when I was four or five years old. I was sitting in the back seat of the cab with my grandmother, and my parents were in the front seat. I guess we went out around Westchester somewhere.

"Look at all the green grass," I said.

"Some day you'll live where there's plenty of it," my mother commented.

Later, I was surprised to see so much grass. The only grass I ever saw around East End Avenue was the kind you see in narrow strips along curbstones. There wasn't any in the playgrounds. Sometimes we went to Central Park, where there was plenty of grass. But that was a public place. The thing that surprised me when my father took us to the country was the amount of grass near people's homes. I couldn't imagine what it must be like to live that way.

But I wasn't sorry for myself, and I wasn't envious. I don't remember ever having said to myself or anybody else, "Gee, I wish I could live like that!" The streets were good enough for me.

One summer—I guess I was five or six—my mother and grandmother actually had a chance to take me to the country for the summer. I think my mother got some kind of a job teaching French on a farm near the Catskills. When I asked her about it later, she said it was wonderful, but it wasn't so wonderful for me. All I remember about the place was a lot of wide open spaces, a couple of big dogs and a shortage of playmates. I couldn't even play stoopball because there weren't any stoops. All I could do was run around with the two dogs. You think talking French to a bunch of American kids is tough? Did you ever try to talk English to a couple of dogs?

I was glad to get back to the slums. But all my mother talked about was getting out of there. Except for the nuns at St. Katherine's, she had no friends there. Neither did my father. He just came and went, doggedly driving his hack and hoping somehow to save enough money for that little house in the country my mother always talked about.

He didn't say much. He let her talk, then went out and worked that much harder. My mother began spending more and more time around St. Katherine's. She taught French to some of the nuns. One of them, Sister Alicia, I think she was called, was very close to the family.

"You will grow up to be big and strong," she said to me once, "but never forget that everything happens only because it is God's will. Without God, you can do nothing. All I want is to serve Him and suffer pain for Him, and I pray that He take me as quickly as possible so that I can join Him in heaven."

2 | *"Breathe!"*

As the years went on, I began to feel as my mother did about moving. It wasn't because I wanted to get out of there either; I think it was because she talked about it so much.

The rides in the country began to take on new significance. We would go along, and my mother would point to a place and say, "I want something like that." Sometimes she would make my father stop, and we would all get out and walk around. But it was some time before we could do anything more than look.

The depression was easing off, and people were starting to ride in cabs again. My father was bringing home more money than he ever had, and we could save a little of it. One day my mother said, "We can afford more rent than we are paying here. Let's go somewhere and stay until we have enough money to buy a house."

We began looking seriously for a place to live. One Sunday we would go to Brooklyn, the next, perhaps, to Yonkers. Some weeks we drove up the Hudson or poked around Forest

13

Hills or looked for places in Jamaica. But for months we couldn't find anything we could afford.

One day we went up beyond Forest Hills, which is the last town on Long Island within the city limits. The next town is St. Albans. Almost as soon as we drove into it, my mother clapped her hands and exclaimed, "This—this is for us! I'm sure we'll find what we want here!"

St. Albans was different from anything we'd seen. In 1939 it had wide open spaces. There were few apartment blocks since almost everyone lived in one- or two-family houses. There were long stretches of land where nobody lived and even some farm country, all of which has long since been built up.

We drove up and down some of the streets, and my mother kept saying, "Roby, breathe deep." I'd breathe deep, and I must admit it didn't smell like the corner of 83rd Street and East End Avenue.

Later she said, "We are going to live here."

That was all right with me, only I hoped I'd find more kids than dogs around.

Three weeks later we rented a small house on 113th Road in St. Albans. The place was tiny, but it was cheap, and there was room for my parents, my grandmother and me. My mother was as excited as a girl. She told everyone she saw about the house in the country where we were going to live. My father was also very happy. St. Albans *was* practically the country yet it was within commuting distance of the city. In his quiet way he showed his happiness.

"You'll like the country," he said to me one day. "You'll never want to live in the big city again."

I had few regrets about leaving East End Avenue. I had memories of fun, but I can't recall any special friends. All of us kids in the neighborhood knew each other, but a boy was never missed if he stopped coming around. There were close family ties but no close ties of friendship. I guess everyone was too busy with his own problems to give more than a passing thought to anyone else.

When I left the East Side, I left it and everyone in it completely. I never went back. I was eleven years old when we moved. I haven't seen the corner of East 83rd and East End Avenue since. The closest I've come is East River Drive. Sometimes when I go by 83rd Street, I experience a flash of recognition but hardly the warm nostalgia that's supposed to be associated with the scenes of childhood.

We drove out of there for the last time in mid-summer of 1939. It was hot and sticky, a perfect day to leave New York City. I remember going over to 83rd Street to say good-bye to the kids, but there weren't any around. I guess they were all on the other side of the fence swimming in the garbage and slime of the river.

A hackie friend of my father's had loaned him a pickup truck, and he had moved the heavy stuff to St. Albans the day before. Now all my father wanted to do was to get us out of there as quickly as possible. The only boy I saw before I left was a kid who lived in the building and went to St. Katherine's with me. We used to walk to school together every morning. He happened to be standing around when we took off. It wasn't a very touching farewell. We just sort of waved to each other, and that was that.

We arrived at the new house on 113th Road about noon. My mother and grandmother were busy trying to get organized, and my father went right to work. I was under foot.

"Go out and play," my mother said. "And don't play in the street. There's plenty of room without going there. Play, and breathe in the wonderful fresh air."

She was right. I didn't have to go to the street. Half a block from the house and facing one side of 113th Road was the biggest playground I'd ever seen, alive with girls and boys of all ages. I couldn't believe my eyes. For a few minutes I just stood and stared.

Kids were actually playing baseball there! Even the school playgrounds in the city weren't big enough for that. They were all small and rectangular. Except for a swing or a slide, they had no equipment. And baseball, which needed plenty of space, was impossible.

But this place in St. Albans was so big that after a while I realized there was more than one ball game going. I learned later that this was O'Connell Playground, and it became my second home. I spent thousands of hours there. I didn't stop going there until I was out of high school.

O'Connell playground was the answer to a kid's—and a parent's—dream. It had play facilities for tiny children, complete with slides and seesaws and swings. There was a baseball diamond, which could also be used for football, and handball courts.

And the first day I saw the place, there was a swimming pool mobbed with youngsters. I didn't know it at the time because it was under water, but when I looked at the pool, I was also getting my first look at a basketball court. When the pool was drained, that was what it was used for. But I was still nearly two years away from the beginning of my love affair with basketball.

I didn't know which way to turn. I just stared for a few minutes, then drifted over to one of the baseball diamonds. When I got a closer look, I saw that the kids who were playing were a little older than I, but after watching them for a while, I didn't think they were any better.

Up to that point, I'd never played in a real ball game in my life. The nearest I'd come to one was stickball. Now I wanted to get into this game, but I was shy about asking so I just watched. Then I heard someone say, "I have to go home."

One of the other kids yelled, "You can't! The game isn't over!"

"I have to," the kid said again.

"What are we going to do for a shortstop?"

"Get another one," the kid said over his shoulder.

I moved in.

"I play shortstop," I said.

"Got a glove?"

I shook my head.

"Here, use mine," a boy on the other team said. And he tossed me a glove.

I ran out to the shortstop's position. Someone threw me a practice grounder. I picked it up and threw to first base. Then someone else yelled, "O.K. Let's go!"

I played all that afternoon and went over and played all the next day before I knew anyone's name.

It wasn't forty-eight hours before I was involved in a violent argument over the relative merits of the Yankees, the Giants and the Dodgers. Most of the kids in the neighborhood hated the Yankees. I was nuts about them. They were always winning, and I liked a winner. I hoped that some day I'd be a winner. I wanted to be a great baseball player and hit like Joe DiMaggio.

When I first started playing in the kids' games around O'Connell, I wasn't very big, but I had those huge hands and good eyes. I had learned how to swing a bat playing stickball, and I was a pretty good hitter. Even though I was one of the youngest kids in the gang, I held my own pretty well.

Most of the kids had bicycles. I lived only half a block from O'Connell, and I had to walk there every day. I didn't mind the walk; I just wanted to have a bike because the other kids had one. So one day, not long after we moved into the house on 113th Road, I said to my mother, "I wish I had a bicycle."

"A bicycle is very expensive, Roby," she said. "I don't think your father can afford to get you one."

"Can I ask him?"

She shrugged, then said with a slow smile, "Asking will do no harm."

So that night when he got home from work, I asked him. He looked at me a moment, then said, "Maybe. Maybe later." He didn't have to say any more. I knew that somehow he'd get me a bike. That's the way he was.

My parents talked about where I would go to school. My grandmother wanted me to go to a parochial school like St. Katherine's. But the only parochial school anywhere near us charged tuition. Aside from that, my mother found out from the neighbors that many of the Catholic children went to public school. Parochial school in St. Albans was either out of our zone or all filled up. She and my father talked it over and decided to let me go to public school. My grandmother wasn't very happy about it, but she accepted the situation.

But even after I began school, she would often sit me down and say, "Roby, some day you must go to a Catholic school."

I would nod my head, wondering a little just how I would ever manage to do what she asked.

"You might go to public school and public high school now," she said one day, "but you must go to a Catholic college."

"Yes, Maman," I said. "I'll go to a Catholic college."

When I first told her that, I didn't know what I was talking about. I was too young to know anything about college except that it cost money, and chances were I'd never have enough to go. But as the years went on, my grandmother never let me forget her wish that I go to a Catholic college. And after a while, I took it for granted that if I ever went to college, it would be to a Catholic one.

In the fall of our first year at St. Albans, I went to P.S. 118, which was at 104th Street, a block off Farmers Boulevard and maybe two miles from my house. It was a long walk, and I began hinting around for the bike again so I could ride it to school. Nobody in the family said much about it, but I didn't want my parents to forget that I wanted one.

I played handball at school. Most of the kids my age did. It was too late for baseball, and I didn't know anything about any other sport. I liked handball because it took only two to play it, and all you needed was a wall. We used to play at recess around school, and then when we got home, we'd play all afternoon. I got to be pretty good at it.

Then about a month after school began, I fell out of a tree and broke my right arm. It was in a cast for weeks. I thought that was the end of the handball games, but one day one of the kids said, "How about a game?"

"How can I play?" I asked. "My right arm's in a cast."

"Use your left," he said.

So I played with my left. He beat my brains out since I couldn't control the ball, but I had a good time. I began practicing by myself and playing whenever I could find someone to play with me. After a while I did a little better. I wasn't beating anybody, but I was winning points. I was developing pretty good control with my left arm.

By the time my right was out of the cast, I was beginning to win some games, using just my left hand. And although no one told me, somehow or other I got the idea that I had something good going for myself. I made up my mind to play with both hands after my right was O.K. again so I wouldn't lose the use of my left.

I played handball all winter. And I walked back and forth to school all winter. I mentioned the bike from time to time but got no reaction from either of my parents. I figured that since they couldn't afford a lot of other things they wanted, they'd never afford a bike for me. So I gave up hope of getting one. But I kept asking on general principles.

Then one day in March when I got home from school, my mother said, "Look in the back yard."

"What's out there?" I asked.

"Never mind," she said. "Just look."

So I walked around the house and looked. There, leaning against the fence, was a shiny bike. I stared at it for a full minute, then walked over and ran my finger along the silver handlebars. They felt cold and smooth and clean.

"Is it mine?" I asked, still incredulous.

"Yes, Roby, it's yours," my mother said.

She was smiling, and there were tears in her eyes. I guess I cried a little myself. This was the one thing I had wanted more than anything in the world, and now I had it.

3 *Morty*

LOOKING BACK NOW, I REALIZE WHAT THAT BIKE MUST HAVE cost my father in work and worry, not to mention money. It was not a new bike, but he had shined it up and fixed the broken parts. I have no idea how long it took him. But he knew how badly I wanted it, and he had made up his mind that I'd have it.

This, I think, was the first really big thrill of my life. That bike meant so much to me that I kept it clean and shiny for years. It lasted me all the way through high school.

Even when we first moved into 113th Road, we knew it was temporary. Right from the start my mother had been saying, "We must buy a house as soon as we can find one within our means." And day after day she and my grandmother looked around the general neighborhood. When my father was home, they drove around in the taxi.

One day, in the summer of 1940, a year after we went to St. Albans, my mother said, "Roby, we're moving."

For a minute, I was scared. But she was smiling so I knew everything would be all right.

21

"Where?" I asked.

"To 116th Road. We bought a house."

The house cost $4,500. My father put his cab in hock to raise the $500 down payment. Then he divided the place up into small apartments so that he could make the monthly payments from the rent. There was a five-room apartment on the first floor, a two-room apartment on the second and a rentable room on the third. My father worked every waking minute he wasn't driving his hack. He fixed up the cellar with a living room and kitchen for us and put beds in the attic. We rented the apartments and crowded ourselves into the rest of the place. For the next few years we all climbed three flights of stairs to go to bed at night.

But my folks were happy because now they had their own home. My mother was so proud that she would sometimes say, "Roby, we are living in our own home! We are property owners!"

The first day I was there, I walked out of the house to ride my bike to O'Connell, which was six blocks away. A short, freckle-faced boy was standing on the sidewalk in front of the house next door. I had seen him around O'Connell, but I didn't know his name.

"Hi," he said.

He grinned, and I grinned back.

"My name's Angus Kennedy," he said. "What's yours?"

"Bob Cousy."

"How old are you?"

"Twelve."

"So'm I. I'll bet we're in the same grade in school. I'm going into the seventh at P.S. 36."

"I'm in the seventh too," I said. "Only I go to P.S. 118."

"Well, you won't go there any more," he said. "They'll make you change. But you'll like P.S. 36."

"I hope I go there," I said.

We got on our bikes and rode over to O'Connell. Angus invited me to play on his baseball team. From then on we were good friends. I changed to P.S. 36, and we went to school together every day. He was my first real permanent friend. And we are friends to this day.

I stuck to baseball until the fall of 1941, when I entered the eighth grade. Now we were only a year away from high school. One day, a boy in my class whom I didn't know too well said, "I wonder how Jackson will do this year in basketball?" and it started a discussion in the schoolyard.

Andrew Jackson High School, where we would all go after we graduated from grammar school, was fairly new and a hotbed of basketball. The coach, Lew Grummond, was considered one of the best on Long Island. Every boy who entered the school wanted to play on the varsity.

When the discussion started in school that day, I realized that I ought to learn something about the game. I was going to Jackson, and I loved all sports. I'd seen the boys play basketball around O'Connell, but I hadn't tried to join them. I was too busy with baseball, and basketball was a game for the older boys. Kids like me didn't have a chance.

"We ought to play basketball," I said later.

"There's a hoop in the schoolyard," Wes Field said. "I'm going to start shooting there."

Wes was a tall, good-looking kid who lived near me. He played baseball with us at O'Connell, and he and Angus and I were buddies. Like Angus, he became a lifelong friend of mine, and we still get together from time to time.

We started hanging around the hoop during recess in the yard at P.S. 36. I'd never before held a basketball in my hands. Once I did, I was hooked.

Nothing very sensational happened the first time I fooled

around with the ball. It felt comfortable in my big hands, but I didn't know how to hold it properly, and I must have looked pretty awkward. All I remember is that the ball went through the hoop, and I got a big kick out of it. But I tried several times after that and missed as often as I hit.

But I loved it. On the way home that afternoon, I said to Angus, "The heck with baseball! From now on I'm a basketball player!"

"Me too," he nodded.

When we went over to O'Connell that day, it was to play basketball. But the court was so crowded we didn't have a chance. The big kids had their usual game going, and there wasn't room for us. I had one or two chances to try to hit with a shot, but I didn't get into a game. Neither did Angus.

But I hung around all day, just waiting for those few chances to get my hands on a ball. Late in the afternoon, just when I was thinking I'd better get home for supper, a short, fat, heavy-set man with curly black hair came over to me.

"You like basketball?" he asked.

I nodded.

"I've been watching you," he said. "I think you could be pretty good."

I didn't say anything.

Then the man said, "By the way, I'm Morty Arkin. I'm the new playground director. I guess we'll see a lot of each other."

I still didn't say anything.

"I know a little bit about this game," he said. "If you need any help, just come around."

"Thanks," I mumbled.

Then he waved and walked away.

I was too shy to go near Morty Arkin for several weeks. But I went down to O'Connell every day, hoping that I'd be

picked to play in one of the games. Wes got picked early because he was taller than we were. Angus and I were little guys,
and nobody paid much attention to us.

Then one day, I ran into Morty, and he said, "Why haven't
you come over to see me?"

"You've been busy," I answered.

"Not too busy for you, son. Your name's Bob Cousy, isn't
it?"

When I nodded, he said, "You're going to be a good basketball player. But you don't know how to shoot."

"I don't?"

"No. Would you like to learn?"

I grinned.

"O.K.," he said. "Look me up when you come around tomorrow."

So the next day, I walked over to him, and he gave me my
first formal lesson in basketball.

"When you shoot," he said, "hold the ball very lightly with
your ten fingertips, not in the palm of your hands. When you
do that, you have no control of the ball."

I had been gripping it with both hands, and I knew he was
right because when I shot the ball in, it was sheer luck. I
never knew if I were going to hit or miss.

"This is a game of accuracy," Morty said. "With fingertip
control, you can develop a high degree of it. So this is basic.
Now try it."

He handed me the ball, and I stood in front of the basket.
I held it by my fingertips, took aim and let it go. The ball
went crazily up in the air, barely reached the hoop and
bounced off the rim.

"That's all right," Morty said. "You'll get it. Say you want
to make a set shot, the kind you'd make from the foul line.
You want full control of that shot. Your natural tendency is

to break your wrists the moment before you throw the ball just as your natural tendency is to grab the ball in the palms of your hands. O.K. Instead of doing that, wait until the exact second you're shooting before you break your wrists. Then you'll always know exactly where the ball is going.

"The thing is—when you make a set shot, you should hit more often than you miss. Sure, sometimes you'll miss because you can't hit every time. But you want to hit as often as possible, and the only way to learn is to shoot correctly."

Before that session was over, he had explained the importance of the follow-through. I knew a little about that from baseball. When you swing a bat, you follow through even after you've hit the ball, and you do the same thing when you throw one.

"In basketball," Morty explained, "the follow-through is even more important than in baseball because it controls the arc of your shot. If you follow through high, you get a soft shot—if low, a hard, bullet shot. And the position of your feet is very important too. When you make a set shot, you keep them close together. Bend your knees according to your distance from the basket. The farther away you are, the more you bend your knees.

All this is basic in basketball, but it was brand new to me. I had never in my life had an older man teach me anything about sports. I had no older brothers, and my father was too busy. Everything I knew I'd picked up from watching other kids.

I was all excited about Morty's willingness to help me. I went over to see him as often as I could. He was always glad to help, and sometimes he even met me after supper.

He encouraged me to learn to shoot with my left hand. It was nearly as strong as my right, although I hadn't stuck too well to my decision to keep using it after my right arm was healed.

Now Morty insisted that I learn to do everything with my left just as well as I did with my right. He knew about the time I had broken my arm and played handball with my left. "That was the best break you ever had," he said.

After he showed me how to make a set shot, he worked with me on layups. This is the easiest shot in basketball, but you have to get in close in order to make it. Once you're there, all you have to do is dunk the ball in. And as Morty pointed out, you have a big advantage if you can do it with either hand because then you can sink the shot no matter which side you use to go in.

He kept after me to drive in from the left side. "It's natural for a right-hander to drive from the right," he said, "but let's say you start in, and that side is so well guarded you see you can't get through. You've got to shift over to the left so that when you do get in you can take your shot with the left hand. If you're a threat from both sides, you'll give your opponent a rough time. He'll never know how to play you."

"Why can't you drive in from the right and shoot with your left, or the other way around?" I asked him.

"You can," he said, "but it's very difficult and awkward. There aren't many guys who can do it, even in college. Maybe some of the pros can, and maybe some day you'll learn how. But when you have your choice of learning the easy way or the hard way, take the easy way. This game is hard enough to learn without making it harder for yourself. So when you want to shoot from the right, drive in on the right. And when you want to shoot from the left, drive in from that side."

I sopped up everything Morty gave me. I practiced morning, noon and night. I started getting up an hour earlier than usual so I could go over to O'Connell and work before it was time to go to school. Sometimes Angus came along with me, and sometimes I went alone, but I didn't miss many mornings. And before I was out of grammar school, I had developed into a pretty good shooter.

Now I was living, eating, sleeping, and dreaming basketball. Angus, Wes and I, along with George Fitzgerald and Don Darnell, a couple of other kids in the neighborhood who were about our age, formed a basketball team and played at O'Connell whenever we could get the use of the court. But that didn't happen often. There were a dozen teams there, and most of them were made up of boys bigger than we were. The only way you could keep the court was to keep winning, and we were too small for that. We'd win once in a while but not often enough to play as much as we wanted to.

We needed a basketball to use at school when we weren't around O'Connell, and Angus came up with a bright idea. The big kids around O'Connell used to let us shoot before their games started and between periods.

"We'll shoot a couple," said Angus, "then we'll swipe the ball."

"How?" somebody asked.

"Very simple," he explained. "We'll set up a relay system. I'll be standing in front of the basket, ready to shoot. Wes, you stand by the fence. Bob, you stand on the other side of the fence. And the other guys will be down the street. Instead of shooting, I'll throw the ball to Wes, he'll toss it over the fence to Bob and Bob'll throw it to one of the others. We'll all run like blazes, and those guys will never catch us."

The scheme was simple and bold. The bigger kids would never dream we had the nerve to pull anything like that, and we'd catch them completely by surprise. We had an added advantage. Angus' older brother played for the big team, and they'd never suspect Angus of double-crossing him. That was why Angus suggested that he begin the chain.

We tried it the next day, and it worked like a charm. We all took our shots as usual, then Angus stood on the line, facing the basket. The older kids weren't even watching him. Suddenly he turned and threw the ball to Wes, who whirled and heaved it over the fence to me. Before the older kids knew what had happened, Angus and Wes had jumped the fence, and we were all running like mad. The ball was a block ahead of us, where Don Darnell, on the end of the chain, was carrying it to a rendezvous at his house.

We kept the ball for three days before the big kids got it back. The only reason they did was because Angus' conscience bothered him. Besides, his brother was on his neck every minute and finally broke down his resistance.

One of the guys on the big team was Ed Ritterbusch. He's now my brother-in-law, and whenever we get together, we laugh about the days when the little kids outsmarted the big ones so they could use a basketball for a few days.

I couldn't get enough basketball that winter. I even went over and shoveled the snow off the yard at P.S. 36 so I could practice at the court there. At night I'd go over and shoot in the dark, taking advantage of a flickering ray of light from a street lamp on Linden Boulevard. It shone on the basket so even though you couldn't see where you stood, you could tell whether the ball went in or not.

I could usually get George Fitzgerald, and sometimes Wes Field, to go over with me. Angus went only when I begged him to.

"I'm crazy about *basketball*," he said, "but I'm not crazy."

But he'd go over when there was something doing at school like an election night or a parent-teachers meeting or a dance or something. Then with the lights on in the building half the court would be lit up, and we could see well enough to get around pretty well.

But the conditions never made any difference to me. In cold weather I'd play and freeze. In wet weather I'd play and get soaked. In the dark I'd play and risk tripping over something and breaking my neck.

I nearly drove my mother out of her mind. "Basketball! Basketball! Basketball!" she would exclaim. "Roby, can't you think of anything else? You'll kill yourself with this game!" (She still says it!)

Angus, Don and I entered Andrew Jackson High in the fall of 1942. George went to a parochial school. Wes Field was half a year ahead of us. By that time basketball was the only thing on my mind. I had visions of taking Jackson High by storm. I'd go out on that floor and kill them. Lew Grummond, the coach, would take one look at me and grab me for his varsity. He would thank his lucky stars for Cousy. I would be the greatest star in the school's history.

Naturally I wouldn't make the varsity right off the bat. I'd be good enough, of course, but there was an unwritten law that freshmen couldn't play varsity basketball. But Jackson had a junior varsity, and of course I'd make that. Then when I was a sophomore, I'd move right up.

I had it all figured out. The trouble was I hadn't tipped Grummond off. When I answered his first call for basketball candidates in early October, I was about as exclusive as a dandelion in a meadow. There must have been 250 kids crowded on the gym floor, and I guess they all looked alike to the coach. He'd already been working with his varsity boys, who came out early on special invitation. This general call was for newcomers and kids who had missed in previous years.

I was five feet, eight inches tall, which is pretty good height for a fourteen-year-old but nothing spectacular for a school-boy basketball player. Grummond was looking for height first, and he more or less automatically picked out the tallest boys.

My first day at practice was my last. I handled a ball twice. Both times I rushed up, dropped in a layup, then got back on the end of a line that stretched from here to there. Kids were dropping in layups all over the place. Grummond would have to be clairvoyant to tell one from another.

He posted the junior varsity squad list a day or so later. We made a dash for the gym as soon as classes were over. When we got to the bulletin board, it was mobbed. We battled through the crowd, and I finally got a good look at the list.

I was the little man who wasn't there. So was Angus. So was Don. The only one in our gang who made it was Wes.

I should have known better than to think I'd stand out in a mob of 250 candidates the first time I went out for the team. I should have known better than to be so disappointed that I couldn't keep the tears from welling up. I should have known better than to think I was one bit better than any of the other kids.

But I didn't. I had my heart set on making the team. In fact, it had never occurred to me that I wouldn't. And while the others milled around, I just stood and stared at the board. It was a long time before I could tear myself away. When I did, I couldn't talk to anybody.

Maybe Angus knew how I felt inside. I'm sure the others didn't. I tried to put up a cheerful front, but I didn't do very well. My mother realized I was unhappy about something, but it wasn't easy to explain to her.

All I could do was sit around for a couple of days and stew. Then Angus said, "It's not the end of the world. So we

don't play for the junior varsity. But there's always O'Connell. And maybe we can get up a team in the Press League.
Anyhow, stop thinking about it."

That afternoon I went over to O'Connell with him, and
we got up a new team without Wes. Once I got on the
court, I forgot my troubles. We won a couple of games that
day and played longer than we'd ever played before.

I felt better too after I had talked to Morty Arkin.

"Don't worry, kid," he said. "You're only fourteen. There's
plenty of time. Sooner or later you'll make the varsity. In the
meantime you've got to practice and practice and practice."

He got me to drive from my left side. "Just shooting from
that side isn't enough," he explained. "If you're a great outside shooter and you can't drive, it doesn't do you any more
good than if you were a great driver and couldn't shoot. You
drive pretty well from the right, and you're shooting from
both sides. But you're a long way from being as good as you
have to be. And you don't drive well from the left."

Morty also made me work on getting the jump on my opponent. I'm not a fast runner, but by getting a quick jump,
I can look like one. As Morty pointed out, that jump is more
important than running speed.

"A half step is all you need," he said. "It can mean the
difference between losing the ball and scoring a basket. After
all, the court is less than ninety feet long. If you steal the
ball at mid-court, you're only a few steps from the basket.

"Everything depends on your first move. You might have
to fake going in one direction and then move in the other.
And if you can move only one way, what good is your fake?
You must never let your opponent know which way you're
going. Make him move first. As soon as he's committed, you
go the other way. By the time he's recovered, you're gone."

Morty also taught me the importance of keeping my body

between my opponent and the ball when I'm dribbling. Actually, dribbling is basic. Any kid who can bounce a ball on the floor can dribble. But the trick is to keep control of the ball. And as Morty pointed out, you've got twice as good a chance of doing that if you can dribble with both hands instead of just one.

I dribbled by the hour with my left. I didn't have full control, but that year I got so I could move the ball back and forth from one hand to the other without breaking the cadence of the dribble. I wasn't dribbling behind my back or setting up any trick stuff, but I was laying the groundwork for it.

❍

In the meantime, we all got involved in various community basketball leagues. Every kid of high school age in Long Island seemed to be playing basketball. There were more leagues than you could keep track of, and I wanted to play in all of them.

The best known loop was the Long Island Press League, run by the newspaper. Everyone was invited to form Press League teams, and we got into the act as fast as we could. We had to pay a ten-dollar registration fee and raise money for uniforms. I got a job delivering fish. This was kind of symbolic, I suppose. I might have smelled a little, but I earned enough dough to get my uniform and contribute to the regisration kitty.

We called ourselves the St. Albans Lindens Juniors and played with other teams in our own age group two or three days a week, sometimes in community houses and sometimes in school gyms. But that wasn't enough for me. St. Pascal's Church, which had been my parish when we lived on 113th

Road, had a Catholic Youth Organization team which played on Sundays. And I also joined the Laureltons, a Jewish team which averaged about one game a week.

I had a good time all winter, and when the leagues folded at the end of the season, I hung around O'Connell and played my share of games. Morty still worked with me, making me polish up everything he had taught me.

"The big thing," he said one day, "is not to be stereotyped. Don't ever be predictable. The minute your opponents learn what you do, they've got you. So be sure you can do something different every time."

He still kept after me to develop my left hand. Among other things, he wanted me to learn to shoot a left-handed hook. A right-handed hook is a natural shot. It's made from the right side close to the basket. You can shoot it in one motion while moving under or away from the basket. It's an effective shot, tricky but essential to a basketball player. I had it down pretty well, but Morty insisted it wasn't enough.

It was years before I mastered a left-handed hook. But I worked on it all during the summer of 1943, and I got so that I could sink the ball with it every so often.

In the meantime, I was enjoying life. We went swimming at Jones Beach, sometimes by ourselves and sometimes with girls. I didn't have any spare cash to spend on dates, but I could always manage an ice cream soda or something.

By the time we went back to school, I was sure I'd attract Lew Grummond's attention in the gym. All that practice paid off pretty well around O'Connell. I was well known there, and the kids used to talk about me by then so I saw no reason to worry.

CHAPTER 4

Twenty-eight points —and a few tears

THE USUAL MOB OF KIDS CAME OUT, AND I GOT LOST IN IT. Just as in my freshman year, it was a matter of standing in line and getting one or two layups in, then maybe scrimmaging a little. I didn't do any more to distinguish myself as a sophomore than I had as a freshman. And I was just as unsuccessful when payoff time came.

It hit me hard enough when I looked at the list and saw that I still hadn't made the junior varsity, but I wasn't as desolate as I had been the year before. By this time, I knew my way around a little better. I was playing in all the community leagues I could and learning fast from Morty Arkin. Sooner or later, I figured, this guy Grummond *had* to notice me. But it looked like it would be later rather than sooner.

I went back to play for the Lindens and St. Pascal's and the Laureltons. We were playing some games in the afternoon and some at night. The Lindens were assigned to the Andrew Jackson Community Center, which turned out to be a good break for me. Lew Grummond became its director that year. He couldn't miss me without deliberately turning his head away, because I'd be in there so much.

It was against the rules to play for more than one Press League team at a time, but I couldn't get enough basketball from my regular three times. So I poked around and finally caught on with another team in a different division from the Lindens.

"You can't be Bob Cousy twice," the manager told me.

"I know it," I said. "I'll play under an assumed name, and just to make sure I don't get caught, I'll disguise myself."

Then I called a girl I knew, Joan Kilduff, who always predicted great things for me, including a varsity berth.

"Can I borrow your name?" I asked her.

"Go ahead," she said.

So I became Bob Kilduff.

My disguise was about as effective as a red flag. When I played as Bob Kilduff, I wore a blue stocking cap with a red pom-pom. I wore it only a couple of times. It was hot and uncomfortable and pretty obvious. I finally got rid of it and regained my anonymity before I got caught.

The Lindens did pretty well. By mid-January we were leading the Class C division of the Press League, and people were beginning to talk about us. I knew that Grummond would eventually see us play so I stopped worrying that I'd never attract his attention.

At that time teams weren't scoring nearly as many points as they do now. There were no speedup rules, and we all played a zone defense instead of a man-to-man. This tended to hold down the scores. A team that averaged 30 points a game was doing well, and anything over that was terrific.

○

The Lindens were hitting 30 points or more regularly, even though we were playing against some teams with older kids.

Our reputation spread all around St. Albans, and one night when we played a contending team, Lew Grummond was watching us.

I noticed him when we were warming up before the game.

"Look who's here," I said to Angus.

"I see," he said.

"Think he'll stay?"

"I hope so."

We all played a good game that night. I didn't do anything that made me stand out, but I scored my share of points. As a matter of fact, once the game began I forgot all about Grummond.

We won by a big score, and as I walked off the floor, Grummond met me.

"Haven't I seen you over at school?" he asked.

I didn't blink.

"Yes, sir," I said.

"What's your name?"

"Cousy. Bob Cousy."

"What year are you?"

"Sophomore," I said.

"You could use a little height," he said.

I didn't say anything to that.

He peered at me a moment, then asked, "Are you left-handed?"

"No, sir," I said. "I'm right-handed."

"Well, you were using your left a lot out there."

"I always do."

"Well," Grummond said, "I like a boy who can use both hands. Come to practice tomorrow. I want to see if you can make the junior varsity."

On the way home, Angus said, "Looks like you're in!"

"Like Flynn," I grinned.

And the next day I was working out with the Andrew Jack

son junior varsity. Grummond put me on the squad, and I played the rest of the season.

It was the first time I'd ever played for a formal team working under a coach with a set system. Up to then we used to make up plays as we went along. Nobody had any definite assignments, and there was no discipline. If you got the ball, you tried to score, and if you couldn't score, you tried to pass it to someone who could. But there was no system and no planned attack of any kind.

Now it was altogether different. Grummond was a strict fundamentalist who had set theories. He knew exactly how he wanted the game to be played. Each man was part of a general pattern, and everyone was expected to do his job and *his* job only. No one was allowed to do anything on his own. The entire emphasis was on team play.

Grummond assigned numbers from one to five to each man. He knew exactly the type of player he wanted for every number. Each year, when he lost men by graduation, he tried to replace exactly those men. At the time he invited me to come to practice, he was looking for a Number One man on the junior varsity.

According to Grummond's system, the Number One man played in a corner and moved across the court on certain plays so that he would be in a position to shoot left-handed layups or short hooks. Because most guys are right-handed, he was always short of Number One men. I got the job because there was nobody else around.

We had a pretty good season. The junior varsity played short games—six-minute quarters—and that alone was enough to keep the scoring down. Sometimes if we started late, we played even shorter periods because we had to leave the floor so the varsity games could start on time. We averaged about 20 points a game and sometimes less. I remember that one night I was the leading scorer with a total of four points.

Grummond was exacting and demanding and hardly my dish of tea, but he was just the type of coach I needed at that stage of my basketball career. Morty Arkin had done a great job of teaching me the fundamentals, but I needed organized coaching.

There was nobody more organized than Lew Grummond. An absolute perfectionist, he demanded nothing short of perfection of everyone else. Even if we won, a fair job was never enough. He could spot flaws as fast as any coach I've ever seen, and he let you hear about them.

Since the junior varsity not only played its own schedule but acted as a foil for the varsity, I got a lot of experience in defensive play. This was something we had never bothered with in the gang. We'd always concentrated on scoring points. We learned how to dribble and drive and shoot in the Press League games, but we didn't know much about keeping the opposing team from doing the same thing.

We learned that winter of my sophomore year. We played more basketball against the varsity than against anyone else. We got so we knew every move the varsity players would make, and we did pretty well defending against them. What was more important, I was getting good training for varsity play.

At the end of the season Grummond said to me, "Bob, you keep practicing all summer. If you improve as much as you should, you'll be on the varsity next season. Remember now, I'm counting on you."

That suited me fine. The guy hadn't noticed me for two years, and now he was counting on me. What more could I want?

‌   ◌

In the fall of 1944 I was ready for the varsity. I had grown a couple of inches and had practiced so hard that the moves were becoming automatic. When Grummond saw me the first day at school, he asked how things were going.

"Fine," I told him.

"Good," he said. "See you in the gym in a couple of weeks."

He saw me in the gym all right but not for long. I managed to get myself into such a mess that I couldn't play varsity basketball until February.

Up to that point, classes were a necessary evil for me. I went to school to play basketball. I was a fair student, but I couldn't be bothered too much with studies. Lew Grummond impressed on us the importance of keeping our marks up so that we'd be eligible for varsity sports, and I figured I was all right as long as I did that. But I forgot that there has to be discipline in the classroom as well as on the basketball court.

All our classes were crowded, but our home rooms were more jammed than anywhere else. That's because we spent the least amount of the time there. The home room teacher took attendance, checked tardiness, listened to excuses, read notes from parents and generally tried to keep order. This was sometimes quite a trick, especially early in the morning before everyone was settled in classroom routine.

Unless we happened to have a home room teacher in a subject, the only mark she could give us was for citizenship.

This wasn't a course (it's called conduct or deportment in other places), though it was just as important as a course. Flunking citizenship was just as bad as flunking math or history.

Our home room was so crowded that there weren't enough desks to go around. As a result, the teacher had to double some of us up. I shared a seat with another boy, and we were so close together that it took some squeezing to make it.

We weren't supposed to talk, which didn't sound like a hardship for me. I was always the great stone face, the guy who never spoke unless spoken to—it says here. Actually, there were times when I couldn't have kept my mouth shut if my life depended on it.

I don't remember my seat-mate's name, but he was a funny little guy who always had a wisecrack on the tip of his tongue. We were together in that seat only half or three-quarters of an hour a day, but it was enough to get me in Dutch.

He'd pull a gag; I'd grin and come up with another, and pretty soon we'd be having a ball—while the teacher went daffy. She warned us half a dozen times, and we'd be quiet for a couple of days, but it never lasted. Sooner or later, we'd be fooling around again.

When it came time for me to report for basketball, I was rarin' to go. I worked hard for a couple of weeks and had the team made. The only possible snag was low marks, but I was studying hard enough to prevent disaster there—at least that's what I thought.

Marks came out in November. I passed all my study courses, but I nearly fainted away when I saw my mark in citizenship. My home room teacher had flunked me!

I rushed up to her.

"You flunked me in citizenship," I said. "Now I can't play basketball."

"I warned you," she said.

"Yes, but I can't play basketball—" I was nearly crying. "Please—I'll never talk to anyone in class again."

"You should have thought of that before," she said.

"You don't know what you're doing to me!" I cried. "Now I can't play basketball! Why won't you let me play?"

"You can play basketball or you can talk in class," she answered sternly. "You can't do both."

"Won't you change my mark—please—this once?"

"No."

Now I was *really* shook up. I rushed over to the gym to see Grummond. I was so close to tears I could hardly talk.

"My home room teacher," I managed to say. "She flunked me in citizenship. Now I can't play basketball. Can't you do anything?"

"Why did she flunk you?" he asked.

"For talking in class."

"Were you talking?"

"Yes," I admitted. "A little."

"Did she warn you?"

I nodded miserably.

"How many times?"

"A couple, I guess."

"Is that all?" the coach asked.

"Well—maybe it was half a dozen or so," I mumbled.

"I see," Lew commented.

He looked at me for a minute. Then he said, "Bob, I need you on the basketball team"—my heart leaped—"but I'm not going to ask that teacher to change your mark." I was desolate again.

"If she hadn't warned you, maybe I'd try to do something," Grummond said. "But she evidently told you repeatedly to stop, and you didn't stop. She had a right to flunk you. If it had been me, I'd have done the same thing."

"But what about my basketball?" I demanded.

"You can work out with the team," he said. "But you can't play until the next marks come out."

"That won't be until February." I was close to tears again. Grummond nodded.

"I know it," he said. "And maybe between now and then you'll learn to keep your mouth shut in the classroom. In the meantime, you can use your spare time most wisely by studying."

I walked away mad. I was sore at the teacher and sore at Lew Grummond and sore at the world. Everybody was against me. And the last person I blamed for my troubles was the guy who caused them all—Bob Cousy.

○

It was a pretty miserable autumn, but it had its points. With not much else to do but study, I hit the books hard and jacked my marks up from the low seventies, where they had reposed for two years, to the low eighties. And I sat back-to-back with my seat-mate, who was as miserable as I was over the whole business. We didn't exchange a word in class for the rest of the year.

I worked out with the team every day, and when the Press League season began, I played for the Lindens again. By the first of the year I was back to normal and looking forward to the end of the term, when I'd be sprung from exile.

This time I passed everything and got an A in citizenship. The high school season was half over. Most of the games, Jackson played had been against opponents of the Queens

Division of the Public School Athletic League, but the boys had a couple of non-league games coming up. We were scheduled to play Bryant High, which was not in the league, the night after I first became eligible.

I was like a coiled spring. I couldn't wait to get on the basketball court. Here I was halfway through my junior year in high school, and I still hadn't played my first varsity game. I thought of those two years I'd missed because I'd gotten lost in the crowd and the third year that I almost missed because I didn't. I had a lot of lost time to make up.

I sank my first basket a minute after the game began, and I was in with another the next time I got the ball in my hands. The other kids realized I was hot, and they all fed me. And Grummond let me do pretty much as I pleased, even though sometimes it was not in his normal script.

I was all over the court that night, dunking in shots from all angles and sinking a couple of long set shots which I probably had no right taking. Anyhow, I ended up with twenty-eight points for the night. It was close to a schoolboy record at the time.

The next morning, I got my first taste of publicity. The Long Island Press had a streamer on the sports page with my name in letters an inch high—COUSY SCORES 28 POINTS. I was thrilled and so were my folks. My mother carefully clipped the story and put it in a scrapbook. It was the first of many for her. Before I was out of high school her first book was full.

Even the New York daily papers mentioned me. All the morning dailies carried short paragraphs about my twenty-eight points. Every time I saw my name spelled out in print, I got a new thrill.

That was the tipoff on a great season for the team. A week or ten days after the Bryant High game we played in Madison Square Garden. I got a huge kick out of that. I had been in the place often, but this was the first time I'd ever played there. I had a pretty good night—I didn't score twenty-eight points, but I went over twenty, as I recall, and we won.

We kept on winning all season and walked off with the Queens Division P.S.A.L. championship. This landed us in the city championships at the Garden. We went all the way to the semi-finals before we got knocked out. En route, we got a million dollars' worth of publicity. By the time the season was over I was fairly well known around town. And at the end of the tournament Chris Werner and I were elected co-captains.

Grummond was delighted with everybody. He had just obtained a job as co-director of a boys' camp out near the tip of Long Island, and he invited a few of us to go with him as counselors. Wes Field, Angus Kennedy, Ray Rasenberger and I all accepted.

I was pretty excited about going there. I was just about to turn seventeen, and I had never been away from home overnight. I looked forward to being with the guys, and I made up my mind I'd work hard and show Lew how much I appreciated his asking me to the camp.

Angus and I shared a bunk. We were in charge of eight kids not much younger than we were—fourteen- and fifteen-year-old seniors. We paid a lot of attention to them until we found out that the camp had waitresses. That was the end of my good intentions. From then on Angus and I paid more attention to the girls than the boys. We had a wonderful time, but we were the world's worst counselors, irresponsible, happy-go-lucky and hard to find. I've got my own camp now, and I'd fire kids who acted as we did then.

It was a great summer for everybody but Lew Grummond. The kids were delighted that nobody was on their necks telling them what to do all the time. We were delighted because of the waitresses. And the girls seemed to be happy. But Lew Grummond was fit to be tied.

It wasn't his camp—he only worked there. We were his responsibility, and we wouldn't have been there if he hadn't invited us. He had sold us to the owners as great kids, the backbone of the Andrew Jackson basketball team that nearly won the city championship. We were minor celebrities and were expected to be friendly with everyone around camp. The only people we were friendly with were the waitresses.

Lew was so mad by the end of the summer that I think he'd have fired us from the team if he could have found a reason for it. But once we got back to school we were all business, and he gradually got over his resentment. But I don't think he ever forgave us, and he never invited us back.

☉

We had just as good a basketball season my senior year as we had the year before. We got off to a fast start, acquired an early lead in the Queens Division and won the title for the second year in a row. For a while we couldn't do anything wrong. We got so far in front that it was pretty obvious nobody was going to catch us.

And this time I hit the jackpot. I scored well from the start, and the other guys helped by feeding me the ball as much as they could. Halfway through the season I was in a dog-eat-dog scoring battle with Vic Hanson of Long Island City.

Neither one of us picked up a long enough lead to stay in front from game to game. When he played and we didn't, he moved ahead. When we played and he didn't, I moved ahead. We seesawed back and forth all season and attracted so much attention around Long Island that folks showed almost as much interest in our battle as in the league race.

On the last day of the season we were in a tie, and we each had one game to go. Long Island City played in the afternoon, and Vic scored twenty-one points. That was his lead as we moved in to play Far Rockaway that night.

My scoring average for the season had been about 17 points a game, and I didn't go over twenty very often. We had the Queens title all sewed up by the last night so the boys agreed to feed me as soon as we took over a safe lead.

I needed feeding. I was tense starting out, and I stayed tense all through the first half. When it was over, I had a whopping eight points. But the other guys did their share of scoring, and we had a pretty good lead when the buzzer went off.

In the second half I was a new man. All the tenseness was gone. I was loose and relaxed, maybe because I figured I didn't have a chance. In any event, the ball started dropping in for me early, and it never stopped. The other guys all helped, and I finished with twenty points for the period and twenty-eight for the night, more than enough to give me the title.

We got knocked out of the city championships in the quarter-finals, and this had us all down for a while. But I was the biggest guy in town the day I was named captain of the city all-scholastic team, which included all five boroughs of New York. Between that and the scoring title, I figured I'd have the whole world to choose from when it came time to pick a college.

5 | *A giant step*

COLLEGE, OF COURSE, HAD BEEN ON MY MIND ALL YEAR. I didn't have money enough to buy my way into a dog-catchers' school, but I didn't see how I could miss getting a scholarship. After all, who would turn down a kid with a record like mine?

Wes Field, who finished high school in February, had already been accepted at Dartmouth. My marks were in the eighties, and I had a vague idea that maybe I'd like to go to Dartmouth too. But I never had the chance; and I'm not sure, for a very good reason, that I'd have accepted.

My grandmother had never stopped talking about a Catholic college. Right up to the day she died she kept reminding me of it. I was perfectly agreeable to the idea, especially since I knew it would have meant so much to her. But I wanted a good Catholic college, one that was away from home and had a campus.

As far as I was concerned, that knocked out Manhattan, Fordham and St. John's, all of which were New York Catholic schools and big basketball centers. Maybe I could have entered one of them or even obtained a scholarship if I'd tried. But I wasn't interested in any of them.

My first thought was to sit tight and wait for the colleges to come to me. Even before the season was over, I expected someone to phone or contact me at school or talk to me at a game or something. But the weeks went by and nobody came around. The college coaches and scouts were avoiding me like the plague. I was six feet tall, but it wasn't tall enough. They were looking for bigger men than I.

◯

Just when I started wondering if I were going to get lost in the crowd again, I got a phone call from Al McClellan, the Boston College basketball coach.

"I came down here especially to see you," he said. "And I'd like to talk to your folks. When will they be home?"

"Tonight," I told him.

"Can I come out then?"

"Sure."

I told my mother about it, and the first thing she asked was, "Is this a Catholic college?"

"A very good one," I said.

That satisfied her. And that night, when McClellan arrived, she and my father were both prepared to like him.

He was an easy guy to like. A huge man, who looked a little like an Arthur Godfrey with salt-and-pepper hair, he had a big grin on his face. The first thing he said was, "Call me Gen—for General. That's what everybody does." Then he began telling us about Boston College.

"We're just starting to build up basketball there," he said. "We're planning a new gym, and we're going to have a top-notch team. And it's a great sports school. That's the place

Frank Leahy got his start. He went from there to Notre Dame."

He talked eloquently for an hour or so. My parents were fascinated. The Gen is a truly charming character, and he didn't spare the horses. By the time he was through, he had my mother and father pretty well sold on B.C., and he had me very much interested. If I would go there, he told us, I would get board, room, tuition and books, and he'd see that I made enough money for any extra expenses. It sounded like a pretty good deal.

He came over to St. Albans again a week or ten days later. This time he brought a plan of the new gym, which he showed us in great detail.

"We're going to start building it this fall," he said. "It'll be ready by the time you're a sophomore."

It sure looked beautiful. The only trouble was that the Gen was about a dozen years ahead of his time. B.C. didn't start building that gym until 1957.

"I'd like to have you and Frank Higgins come back to Boston with me and look over the college," he said. "I think you'll like it."

"Go ahead, Roby," my mother said, "and if you like Boston College, you should go there."

So Frank Higgins, who also played at Andrew Jackson, went to Boston with me a few days later. The Gen met us, and we got the red carpet treatment. He showed us around the lovely B.C. campus, which is high on a hill overlooking the city, and I was deeply impressed with its Gothic towers. I met John Curley, the graduate director of athletics, and Father Maurice Dullea, the faculty moderator, and all the guys on the basketball team.

Except for one thing it was all pretty impressive, but that one thing was enough to steer me away. For all B.C.'s stately beauty, it lacked a campus dormitory. It was essentially a day school; practically all the students commuted. And if I had gone there, I would have lived in a rooming house nearby.

This I couldn't see. If I was going to a day school, I'd stay in New York. But I didn't tell the Gen that. When he asked me what I thought, I told him everything was dandy but I just hadn't made up my mind.

"As soon as I do, I'll let you know," I said.

Then Higgins and I went home to St. Albans. Frank, incidentally, finally did join the Gen at B.C.

Right after I got home from that trip, I got a phone call from Ken Haggerty. He lived in St. Albans and had once been a basketball star at Andrew Jackson High. He had then entered Cornell and later tranferred to Holy Cross College in Worcester, Massachusetts, where he was a junior.

"Have you decided where you're going to college?" he asked.

"No," I said.

"Well, I'd like to drop over and tell you about Holy Cross."

"Come ahead."

○

The more Ken told me about the place, the better I liked it. Holy Cross was a Catholic school, and like B.C., its traditional rival, it was run by Jesuit priests. It had a hilltop campus, excellent scholastic standards and was primarily a dormitory school.

Until that year it had never done much in basketball. Up to 1939, it had dropped the sport three times. From 1939 to 1945 the team had won only twenty-two games. There'd been no basketball court and no gym, and the boys had practiced in an old barn.

But in 1945 Holy Cross hired a new coach, Alvin (Doggie)

Julian. He was also end coach of the football team, but his
first love was basketball, and he wasted no time building up
a team. Before starting his first season, he brought in half a
dozen outstanding boys from the Greater New York area,
guys like Dermie O'Connell, George Kaftan, Joe and Dave
Mullaney and Haggerty. And with this nucleus Julian built
up a team which attracted 166,000 fans during the 1945-46
season. Holy Cross had sold out the Boston Garden twice that
year, and since the backbone of the ball club was made up of
freshmen, the best was yet to come.

"It sounds great," I said. "Will they give me a scholarship?"

"We'll be in town soon," Ken said. "Then you can talk to
Doggie."

About ten days later, Haggerty phoned to invite me to sit
on the Holy Cross bench when they played Kings Point at the
Jamaica Armory that night. He called for me early and after
we arrived at the armory, took me into the locker room and
introduced me to Julian and the boys on the team.

"I've heard a lot of nice things about you," Doggie said.

I mumbled an embarrassed "Thanks."

Then Doggie said quietly, "Let me tell you about Holy
Cross."

He talked for half or three-quarters of an hour. He didn't
say much about the team, but he described the college in
great detail—its appearance, location, the kind of boys who
go there, the high scholastic requirements, the faculty and
the dormitory life.

"Your marks are good," he said. "I don't think you'd have
any trouble getting in."

He didn't pressure me, but he didn't have to. I liked everything about the place—Doggie, the boys, the uniforms, even
the name Holy Cross, which was so obviously Catholic. Dog-

gie promised to send me pictures of the campus as well as catalogs and all the papers that would have to be filled out if I were to apply for admission there.

After the game he pulled me aside again.

"Are you considering any other college?" he asked.

"Well," I told him, "I'm thinking about B.C. They've offered me a scholarship."

"What kind?" Julian asked.

"Board, room, tuition and books," I said.

"I think we might do the same for you," he told me.

I was sold, but I didn't commit myself then. I wanted to wait until Doggie sent me all the stuff he promised. Besides, I had to convince my parents. They liked the Gen, and they wanted me to go to B.C.

We had several discussions about it, but they all came down to the same thing—Holy Cross had dormitories, B.C. didn't.

"But that Gen is such a nice man," my mother kept saying. She and my father finally came around.

"You really want Holy Cross, don't you?" she said one day. I nodded.

"All right," she said. "We shouldn't try to interfere. You go to Holy Cross."

I filled out the application that night along with a letter to Doggie, telling him that I'd accept a scholarship offer from Holy Cross. A few days later he made it official.

In the meantime, a few of the Andrew Jackson boys had been invited to scrimmage against the Brooklyn College basketball team. We went over there several times and did very well against the college boys.

One day their coach, Artie Musicant, took Wes Field and me into a corner and said, "What are you guys doing this summer?"

Neither of us had any definite plans. The only thing we were sure of was that we weren't going back to camp with Lew Drummond.

"How would you like to come up to Tamarack Lodge with me?" he said.

6 *Hoops and hoopla*

TAMARACK LODGE IS IN THE HEART OF THE BORTSCH BELT, A huge colony of summer resorts in the Catskill Mountains. It attracts a heavy concentration of people from New York, many of whom are crazy about basketball. The biggest resorts offer all sorts of entertainment for their guests, and no bortsch belt entertainment program is complete unless it has its own basketball team.

Every big place had a team, and a pretty active recruitment program went on during the spring. Boys from colleges all over the East played in the bortsch belt, and some of the top coaches in the country worked there.

The boys were given jobs as waiters and bus boys so they could maintain their amateur standing. The better the place, the higher the tips, and Tamarack was considered one of the top resorts. Artie Musicant was the athletic director there, and his invitation was all we needed.

"I don't know about you, Wes," I said, "but I just joined the bortsch belt."

"Me too," Wes said.

Between Dad's taxicab and the rent we were collecting, the family finances were in better shape than usual. When I told my dad about going to Tamarack, he said in his quiet way, "You'll need a car."

"How can I get a car?" I asked.

"I'll give you $300 towards one."

I bought an ancient heap and drove it up to Tamarack. Three weeks later it was in the ashcan.

Six of us piled into it one night to take a ride over to Ellenville. I was hitting it up pretty well on one of those mountain roads, with nothing between the edge of the road and the foot of the mountain except air, but nobody was worried, least of all me.

We went barreling along down the incline when we suddenly came to a sharp turn I'd forgotten about. Before I could bring the wheel around, the car scooted off to the side, and while I frantically tried to keep it in control, shot through the guard rail and started turning over in slow-motion.

I thought we'd all cash in our chips, and I'm sure we would have except for a colossal break. There just happened to be two trees growing out of the mountainside at that point, and we crashed right into them after turning over one and a half times. I hadn't had brains enough to drive more carefully, but I did have the wit to turn off the ignition so the thing wouldn't catch fire. Then I looked around to see if anyone was alive.

One guy after another crawled out through a hole in the canvas roof, and each one was operating under his own power. We all climbed back up to the road and checked each other for broken bones. Nobody had any. The worst any of us suffered were a few scratches and cuts.

o

Tamarack Lodge was what they call a five-and-three house up in the bortsch belt. That meant the customers were advised to tip the waiters five dollars a week and the bus boys three. Of course, nobody could force anyone to tip anything, but most people followed the recommendations.

In my first year there, I was a bus boy. My job was to set and clean up the tables and help the waiter by keeping the water glasses filled and making sure there was enough bread and butter—when they served butter—on the tables. Like most resorts in the Catskills, Tamarack was a kosher house so butter was never put on the tables when there was a meat course.

I wasn't familiar with the situation, but I learned fast. The first day I was there I asked the waiter why we didn't put butter on the tables.

"Young man," he said, "I see you have a lot to learn. Listen carefully while I tell you the facts of life up here."

He then gave me a concentrated ten-minute course in the dietary laws. I asked no more questions after that, and for the rest of the summer I lived a kosher life.

We played two basketball games a week, one at home and one away. Doesn't sound like much, but it was actually a pretty rugged schedule. We had practically no free time in the morning. By the time the breakfast dishes were cleared up, it was nearly time to set the tables for lunch. We'd have maybe three-quarters of an hour in between.

The afternoons were better because once lunch was cleared away, we'd have two and a half or three hours. I spent most of the time either on the basketball court or at the swimming pool. Sometimes I played handball.

That was the year I first got seriously interested in tennis. I always liked the game because it's a great conditioner for the legs, but I had never played it much. At Tamarack practically everybody played it. I spent a lot of time on the courts, and I've been playing a good deal of tennis since. I even got into a few tournaments later. And in the summer of 1957 I went down to Brookline, Massachusetts, from my camp and conducted a tennis clinic for kids.

The nights we didn't play basketball at Tamarack were our own, and we made good use of them. We didn't have to stir out of the place to find dates; there were plenty of girls right on the premises. I had fully as good a time there as I'd had at the camp on Long Island, and I didn't have to travel half as much.

The basketball league was a tough one. George Mikan, a pro then, and Ed Macauley, Dolph Schayes, Donnie Forman, Ziggy Bank and Bill Rosenblatt, all great college players at the time, were on various teams. Macauley and Schayes later became outstanding professional stars. Ziggy was with us.

There was only one thing wrong with bortsch belt basketball—the betting was too heavy. We had an unhappy experience my second year there that scared us all, although it helped cut down the gambling.

We were playing a home-and-home series with another resort. We lost the first game, but that was on a strange court, and we figured we'd murder these guys when we played them at Tamarack. But that game smelled to high heaven. Ziggy, Wes, and I all had big nights—Ziggy had twenty-two or twenty-three points, Wes had about twenty, and I had twenty-five or twenty-six—but no matter what happened, the other team always stayed ahead of us. Under ordinary conditions, we should have won, but we took a bad beating. We were licked by fourteen or fifteen points.

We found out later that by half-time the crowd had heard that something was fishy, but we didn't know it. All we knew was that we were beating our brains out and losing the ball game.

As soon as it was over, we were called into a huddle with Dave Levinson, Tamarack's owner. He had information that a couple of our players were in on a betting coup. One of the employees had confessed that he was the liaison man between the players and a hotel guest who had bet a bundle on the other team. Levinson fired the players and the hotel employee, and the guest got his walking papers on the spot.

That was the first time I'd ever heard of ballplayers dumping games for gamblers. Three years later the college betting scandal broke. I've often wondered if the guy who pulled the strings at Tamarack was mixed up in that too.

I was in pretty good shape financially after that first summer at Tamarack. I banked some money, and gave the rest to my folks. It was the least I could do in view of the fact that I'd poured nearly $300 of my father's hard-earned money down that mountainside.

7 | *Holy Cross*

MY HEART GAVE A TUG WHEN I SAID GOOD-BYE TO THE FAM-
ily and the gang around St. Albans the day I left for college.
I was taking a midnight train which was due in Worcester at
seven in the morning. This college business was something
brand new and it upset me a little. I was leaving old friends
and facing the prospect of having to make a whole set of new
ones in a place farther away from home than I'd ever been
before.

On top of that I had to make the trip alone. Ken Haggerty,
the only Holy Cross man I knew, didn't have to report to college for several days. I sat up all night on the train, feeling
sorrier and sorrier for myself. And when I got my first look
at Worcester, I wanted to turn around and go right back to
New York.

I walked through the dingy old railroad station as fast as I
could, and when I got to the street, I couldn't see how a tree
could grow there, much less a whole college. All I could see
were grimy buildings that made the East Side of New York
look like Bar Harbor. There didn't seem to be any boys about

my age who might be headed for Holy Cross. The only people I saw were in a bleary-eyed rush to get to work. Nobody
paid any attention to me. I felt like a yokel. More than anything else, I had an overwhelming desire to see St. Albans.

I felt a little better after I got into a taxi and headed for
the college. The town didn't look much better to me—we
went through an industrial area which looked even worse
than it was because of the hour and a dull, steady rain. But
at least I was on my way.

And when I first saw the Holy Cross campus, I was back
in shape. I always get a thrill out of the place, but I don't
think I ever got as big a charge as when I saw it for the first
time. The cab turned into the grounds, high on a hill, and
went up a tree-lined road leading to the main buildings. On
my right was a steep, still green lawn. At the foot of the hill,
Fitton Field, the football stadium, stood out in sharp relief.
Everything was okay. I was going to like this place.

꙳

The taxi let me off in front of the administration building,
and I walked in to register. It was early, but plenty of guys
were around. I was still lonesome, but I knew I'd meet somebody sooner or later. And in the meantime, all I wanted to
do was find my room, wash off the railroad dirt and take a nap.

But it was an hour or so before I got into my room. A
trunk and an open suitcase were the first things I saw, but
there was no sign of my roommate. Later when he walked in,
I was just getting ready to sack out.

"My name's Bill Feeney," he said.

I shook hands and introduced myself.

"What's your sport?" he asked.

"Basketball," I said.

He looked disappointed. "I'm a track man," he said. "I don't know anything about basketball."

"That makes us even," I said. "I don't know anything about track."

It was hardly a rousing start, and it got worse before it got better. Bill, who later became a good friend of mine, lived in Rhode Island and he couldn't wait to get back there. Classes weren't due to begin for three or four days.

After he got his stuff put away, he said, "Well, see you later"—and off he went.

Now I really felt sorry for myself. And I didn't even have a roommate to commiserate with.

I spent the next couple of days poking around the place. Except for the football squad, there were no upperclassmen around, and most of the freshmen seemed to have crawled into cubbyholes of their own.

I ran into Doggie Julian my first day on the campus.

"Are you all settled?" he asked.

"Fine," I said.

"Good. I know you'll like it here. I wish I could spend a little time with you, but I'm busy with football."

"That's all right," I said. "I'll get along."

"I'll let you know when we start basketball practice," he added. "You know, we're still on wartime rules here. Freshmen are eligible for the varsity. I'm looking forward to seeing you on the squad."

I thanked him, and we passed the time of day for a few minutes longer. Then he headed for the football field. Except for a quick hello here and there, that was the last I saw of him for weeks.

With not much else to do, I wrote a lot of letters—to my folks, to Joan Kilduff, with whom I was still going, to the guys, and when I got through, I wrote more letters. Joan heard from me more times my first two days at Holy Cross than she did all the rest of the year.

Bill Feeney came back the day before classes began.

"Say, Bob," he said, "I wonder if you'd do me a favor."

"Sure."

"I've got a buddy in another room," he said. "He's a track man, and the two of us would like to be together. Do you mind swapping with him?"

"Not a bit," I said. "I think it's real nice that you track men want to be together."

My new room was right around the corner. When I walked into it, a huge guy was stretched out on a bed. When he got to his feet, he seemed to stand up in sections. He towered over me by a good three inches.

"My name's Al McAvoy," he said, holding out a big hand.

I introduced myself, then said, "McAvoy? Are you the McAvoy from Brooklyn Prep?"

He nodded.

"I've heard of you," I said.

"I know all about you too," he remarked.

Al McAvoy was a baseball pitcher who could have jumped right from prep school to the Dodgers if he'd wanted to. He got plenty of publicity around New York because he turned down a huge bonus in order to go to Holy Cross.

While we were talking, a heavy-set boy walked in.

"We've got a new roommate, Mike," McAvoy said. "Meet Bob Cousy. Great basketball player. Bob, this is Mike Boyle. Great football player. You guys ought to get along all right."

As it turned out, all three of us got along all right. We were roommates throughout our entire college careers.

Things were looking up. Gradually, as the days went on, I

started to run into other basketball players. The team hadn't
been brought together, but the guys looked each other up as
a matter of course.

A week after I entered Holy Cross, Dermie O'Connell
grabbed me in the lunch room and said, "Come over here.
I want you to meet a guy who doesn't play basketball but is
practically a member of the team."

I followed him to one corner of the room. Seated at the
table was a stocky boy with curly brown hair and a friendly
smile on his face.

"This is Bill Gallagher," O'Connell said. "Bill, shake hands
with Bob Cousy."

Before I could reach my hand out, Bill stood up and prof-
fered his. His grasp was firm, and his smile was warm.

"Glad to know you, Bob," he said. "I've heard a lot about
you."

Then he sat down, and I pulled out an empty chair. We all
talked through lunch, and Bill joined in as one of the gang. It
wasn't until we got through eating and he stood up and
reached for Dermie's arm that I realized he was blind.

Gallagher was Mr. Basketball while he was at Holy Cross.
He made every trip with the team, had a place in the locker
room and on the bench during games. The boys took turns
telling him what was going on. He was a pleasure to have
around, and I missed him when he graduated a year ahead
of me. He is now a highly successful social worker in Newton,
Massachusetts.

☉

I didn't see much of Doggie Julian during those early
weeks at college, but I heard a lot about him and what he
had done to revive basketball in New England. The game

was invented there when James A. Naismith attached a couple of peach baskets to a gymnasium balcony in Springfield, Mass., in 1891. It may have been popular around New England for a while, but the sport didn't last. Up to 1945 New England was a basketball graveyard.

Except for Rhode Island State and Dartmouth, there hadn't been a good college basketball team in New England in many years. Even those two clubs couldn't draw flies in Boston, where the big winter sports were ice hockey and track. No more than 1,500 people had ever watched a basketball game in Boston before Julian went to Holy Cross.

Doggie and the team he brought in sold the sport in less than a year. By the time I entered Holy Cross in the fall of 1946, New England sports fans were daffy about the Crusaders. Joe Mullaney, Dermie O'Connell, Charlie Bollinger, Ken Haggerty, Bob Curran and George Kaftan were household words. Frank Oftring, Andy Laska and Matty Forman all entered college with me, and we were all brought in by Doggie.

The first team Julian had was made up of O'Connell, Mullaney, Haggerty, Kaftan and Curran, and these guys had had a great year. They played a number of their "home" games in the Boston Garden, and with the help of Boston newspapers, which had ignored basketball up to then, they had built up a tremendous following.

There wasn't a chance for a newcomer to break into that lineup, but I didn't have the sense to realize it. If I had, I would have saved myself a lot of grief. I thought I was the world's greatest basketball player and that there wasn't a team I couldn't make. After all, hadn't I been captain of the New York City all-scholastic team the year before? And hadn't I just finished a summer playing against some of the best college players in America? And didn't I have all the shots and know all the moves and have all the physical equipment? How could this guy Julian overlook me?

Actually he didn't, but I thought he did. Doggie told us the first day of practice that he expected to platoon the squad. The first platoon would be made up of his regular team of the year before. The second would be recruited from among Laska, Oftring, Bollinger, McMullen, Dennis O'Shea and myself. All I had to do to see that this added up to six was count on my fingers.

The great Cousy was going to have to fight for a job on the *second* platoon. This, I thought, was adding insult to injury.

Actually, there was never any doubt about my making the second platoon. Doggie had no intention of leaving me off it. But I didn't know that, and I made no attempt to find out. I simply came out to practice, worked when I had the chance and stewed on the bench when I didn't.

I should have gone to Doggie then and tried to reach an understanding with him. Instead I sulked. I was mad, and I made no attempt to hide the fact. And I'm sure that when Doggie realized that I resented not playing on the first team, he resented my resentment. The seeds of a first-class feud had been planted. And that first year at least, practically every seed was planted by Cousy.

8 | *Doggie*

WHATEVER TROUBLES I HAD WITH DOGGIE JULIAN WERE ninety per cent my own fault. As the weeks wore on, I built up a great case for myself. Doggie, of course, gave the bulk of his time to his first team. The old barn where we practiced was narrow, and there was hardly room for two teams to work at once. So Doggie set up his patterns with the first team, and after working with them at some length, he turned his attention to us. In the meanwhile, we sat around and watched.

The longer I postponed going to Doggie to try to hash things out, the worse the situation became. I sulked by myself and confided in nobody, not even my roommates. I felt so sorry for myself that I took to stopping in at chapel after practice and praying for Doggie to give me the chance I wanted. I got some solace from that and always felt better when I walked out. Yet I would go through the same thing all over again the next day.

The season began, and the first team really went to town! They started the games, and they were on the floor for long periods of time.

If I'd stopped to think about it—which I didn't—I would have seen that the ends justified the means. Julian was the coach, and it was his job to win. And whether I was on the bench or not, the fact remained that we were winning.

Furthermore, I *was* getting plenty of action. I really had no squawks. For a freshman, I was doing all right. I had a third of a game here, half a game there. And Doggie was letting our platoon do pretty much as it pleased. Laska was a great ball-handler, and he and I pulled off some razzle-dazzle stuff that resulted in scores. The crowd loved it, and Doggie didn't seem to mind.

Sometimes he moved George Kaftan in with us. Kaftan was the highest scorer in Holy Cross history at the time. He was the top banana of the ball club. If I'd stopped to think things out, I would have realized that Doggie's moving him in with us was proof enough what he thought of us. He wanted us to get experience playing with Kaftan, who still had two years to go after this one.

We rolled along and went into a terrific winning streak. As we knocked off one opponent after another, the fans of Boston and New England went crazy. They poured into the Garden to see us pile up our string of victories. Before we were stopped, we had won twenty-three straight games, and we ended the season with a record of twenty-seven wins and only three defeats.

If I had bothered to look up the records, I would have found that Doggie had let me play often enough to score 227 points, only ten less than Kaftan had scored the year before. I couldn't possibly have scored them all from the bench.

We went into the N.C.A.A. tournament in New York as the Cinderella team of college basketball. And playing his strength—his first team—most of the way, Doggie led us right to the championship. We beat Navy, C.C.N.Y. and

Oklahoma in succession in a series which found Kaftan so hot
that he could have been elected governor of Massachusetts
if he'd wanted it.

The conquering heroes came home to Worcester, and Cousy
was just another guy. I had played about a third of the Navy
game but had entered only in spots during the rest of
the tournament. I was glad we won, but I wished I'd had more
to do with it.

And I was madder than ever at Doggie Julian.

○

When we got back to Worcester, I really made a chowder-
head of myself. I wrote to Joe Lapchick, who was then the
basketball coach at St. John's University in Brooklyn. I told
him I was unhappy at Holy Cross and discouraged about the
future. I said I wanted to transfer to St. John's and asked him
if he'd help me do it.

Lapchick answered me by return mail. I didn't save the
letter, but as I remember, it went something like this, in part
at least:

"You're not in college primarily to play basketball but to
get an education, and you're getting a very good one at Holy
Cross. And if you should transfer to St. John's, you wouldn't
be gaining anything in that respect.

"Doggie Julian is one of the finest basketball coaches in
America, and some day you'll be proud you've played for him.
He doesn't want to hurt you and isn't doing so deliberately. I
know he is depending heavily on you in future years and
would be very much upset if he knew how you felt.

"Aside from everything else, transferring from one college
to another is at best a risky move. You don't know if you're
going out of the frying pan into the fire. And college rules

dictate that you must wait a year before being eligible for varsity competition. This would hardly make it worth while for you.

"Be patient. You're only a freshman. Your turn will come. Stay at Holy Cross. You'll never regret it."

To this day, I'm grateful to Joe Lapchick for that advice. I've often wondered since how many other coaches would have offered me the same words of wisdom.

I told only one person about my letter to Lapchick and Joe's answer. That was a priest at Holy Cross named Father Bean. I knew him only casually. I used to see him around at practice and during some of our games.

He met me on the campus the day after I got Lapchick's answer.

"You're Bob Cousy from the basketball team, aren't you?"

"Yes, Father," I said.

"I hope you don't think I'm intruding, but I've noticed you seem very unhappy," he said. "Is there something on your mind?"

"Well, to tell you the truth, Father—" I began. Then I hesitated.

"Would it help if you told me about it?" he said gently.

Then suddenly it all spilled out. I told Father Bean everything—about my hopes when I first entered Holy Cross and my first day at practice and how Doggie wouldn't change his first team and how I resented being ignored and not being able to make myself go to him and all the other things that had happened during the year, including my decision to leave Holy Cross and my correspondence with Lapchick.

And when I got all through, Father Bean said, "That St. John's coach must be a fine man. He gave you wonderful advice. I hope you intend to follow it."

"I do, Father," I said.

"Really, Bob," the priest said, "when you stop to think about it, things aren't as bad as you imagine them."

And when I stopped to think about it, I realized that this whole thing was all in my mind. I'd got myself into this stew, and Doggie probably wasn't even aware that I was in it.

○

I made up my mind to change. Next year, when I came back as a sophomore, I'd love everybody, including Doggie.

But it wasn't easy when the fall of 1947 rolled around. I was a little apprehensive because I hadn't exchanged a word with Doggie since the end of the previous season. I hadn't looked him up to say good-bye when I left school at the end of my freshman year, and I didn't look for him to say hello when I came back in the autumn.

I did run into him shortly after school began. We shook hands and he said, "We'll have a good year. See you when practice starts."

Things seemed to go very well at practice. Doggie didn't have much to say to me, but he used me much more than he had the year before. It looked as if our troubles were over.

In the meantime, I had become very friendly with the new Moderator of Athletics, Father John F. Tiernan. He was a great fan, and basketball was his favorite sport. He came over to practice often, and he and I got into the habit of talking basketball together. I told him how anxious I was to play and later gave him some idea of how I had felt the year before.

Everything went fine at the start of the season. Doggie was using me regularly now, pairing me up with Kaftan. The two of us made a good combination. The club needed help. We had lost Curran and Haggerty, and we lacked experience.

But we were winning our share of ball games, and we seemed headed for a good season.

Doggie and I had little to say to each other. While most of my grievances of the previous year had all been in my mind, there was no question of a personality clash. I couldn't put my finger on the trouble spot, and I'm sure Doggie couldn't either. We just didn't like each other. But we got along on the surface, and everything seemed to be going along fine until mid-December. Then the roof blew off.

We were facing one of the biggest games of the year against Loyola on a Tuesday night at the Boston Arena. In preparation for this big one, Doggie scheduled one practice session at one o'clock Sunday afternoon and another Monday night.

On Saturday, I had been invited to a dance at a girls' school about two hours' drive from Worcester. I left that afternoon with a couple of other guys, neither of them basketball players. We went to the dance, then got up Sunday morning in time for early Mass so that we could get back to Worcester in plenty of time for me to make that one o'clock practice session.

We went along fine for an hour or so. But with another hour of driving ahead of us, we skidded in the snow and barged into another car. Nobody got hurt, but there was plenty of body damage to both cars.

We killed an hour and a half exchanging licenses and registrations and arguing over whose fault it was and getting the damage repaired, at least temporarily. And when we finally got started for Worcester again, my one o'clock date with Doggie and the team was long gone. On top of that, we had to drive more slowly because it had started to snow again. It was four o'clock in the afternoon before we got back to the campus.

I jumped out of the car and rushed for the barn where we

practiced. On the way, I ran into Father John Devlin, a priest who was such a hot basketball fan that he used to take action and team pictures.

"Hello, Bob," he said. "We missed you at practice."

"I know, Father," I said.

"What happened?"

"We were driving home from a dance this morning, and we got into an accident," I said. "Nobody got hurt, but there was some damage to both cars, and we were delayed. Gee, Father, I'm really upset. Is Doggie around?"

The priest shook his head.

"He left some time ago," he said. "There's nobody around now."

"Well, what can I do?" I asked.

"I don't think you can do anything," Father Devlin said. "Go up to your room and forget about it. And tomorrow you can explain what happened."

I went to my room, but I didn't forget about it. I knew Doggie must have been mad, and I hoped he'd accept my explanation. But the next morning, after I happened to meet Frank Dooley, the team manager, in class, I didn't have much hope.

"What happened to you?" he asked.

I told him.

"Have you told Doggie?" Frank inquired.

"I haven't seen him," I said. "I got back too late yesterday."

"He's wild—mad as hell. He thinks you played in an outside game yesterday."

"But I went to a dance," I said.

"Tell him about it," Frank said. "Maybe everything will be okay."

As soon as classes were over, I went looking for Doggie,

but he wasn't anywhere around. Now I was really anxious to tell him what had happened. I couldn't have him thinking I'd played in an outside game for that was strictly against the rules.

When I couldn't find Doggie, I went to Father Devlin.

"I don't know where Doggie is," he said, "but I'm sure I'll see him later in the day."

"Will you tell him what happened?" I asked.

"I'll be glad to," the priest said.

I didn't see Doggie until practice that night. Father Devlin told me then that he had explained the situation to Doggie, but I wanted to tell him too.

Doggie ignored me during practice. I didn't even get into a scrimmage. He just let me sit and burn. And every time I went near him, he turned and walked the other way.

After practice I rushed up to his office and waited for him. When he walked in, I said, "All right, Doggie. Let's get this into the open. I missed practice yesterday, and I'm sorry. Do you want to hear what happened to me?"

"No, no, no," he said. "I don't want to hear anything."

Then he turned and walked out. I caught up with him in the outer hall.

"Look, Doggie," I said. "I haven't done anything wrong. Won't you let me explain?"

He shook his head, then pushed past me and walked away.

Now I was frantic. I went to Father Tiernan and told him the whole story. He, in turn, talked first to Father Devlin and then to Doggie. And later Father Tiernan called me into his office.

"Bob," he said, "he won't believe anything. He's convinced you played in an outside game instead of going to practice, and I can't make him change his mind."

"What can I do?" I asked.

"I haven't the slightest idea," Father Tiernan said. "He's just awfully angry. He told me he won't play you in the Loyola game tomorrow."

That practically prostrated me. I dragged myself back to my room and went to sleep half hoping I'd never wake up.

The team met at the gym after an early dinner, and we all piled into a bus for the thirty-five mile ride to Boston. I tried to talk to Doggie again, but he wouldn't pay any attention to me. I wanted to sit with him in the bus, but there wasn't room. And after we arrived at the Arena, I still couldn't get near him.

The game was an Arena sellout—one of the biggest of the year. Loyola had a great team, and it would mean a lot to us to win. I couldn't believe that Doggie meant what he said when he told Father Tiernan he wouldn't play me, but when he called the starting lineup together, I wasn't in it. And as the first half progressed and replacements were needed, he skipped over me.

The longer I sat on the bench, the madder I got. And when the half went into its final stages and he still hadn't called on me, I muttered to myself, "The hell with him! The hell with him! I wouldn't go in now if he asked me!"

Ten seconds later he did. Without looking at me, he called, "Cousy!"

There were thirty seconds left in the half. To me, this was the height of humiliation. I sat tight. I refused to go in for thirty seconds.

Wrong? Sure, I was wrong. After all, I was on the team, and he was the coach. But I had one thing going for me. The guy hadn't given me the same hearing a judge would have given a suspect. And if I was sore, I felt I had a right to be.

I sat in the locker room between the halves and moped. The

rest of the guys were just lying around taking it easy, saving their strength for the second half. The game was very close, and they'd need everything they had to win it.

Doggie didn't have much to say. He talked for a few seconds just before it was time to go out again. He paid no attention to me, and I didn't look at him. And when we filed out for the second half, I buried myself in the middle of the line and carefully found a seat on the end of the bench, as far away from Doggie as I could get.

The second half got under way, and as it progressed, it began to look as if we were going to lose it. At the halfway point, Loyola had a slight lead, and that increased as the final quarter got under way.

I sat watching and quietly praying that we'd pull this out somehow. Doggie still hadn't put me in. I figured he wasn't going to now, even if it cost us the game. I was just hoping that the other guys could do the job.

Now there were only five minutes to go, and Loyola had a six- or seven-point lead. Our guys were dished, dragging themselves around the court, trying to keep things under control but not succeeding too well.

Then from off in one corner of the Arena, I heard a couple of guys yell, "We want Cousy! We want Cousy!"

At first it was just an isolated yell, but somebody in another part of the place picked it up, and after a few seconds it swept across the Arena, a deeply swelling chant that quickly developed into a roar.

"WE WANT COUSY! WE WANT COUSY! WE WANT COUSY!"

Goose pimples started creeping along my spine. By this time, it seemed as if all the people in the joint—about 8,000— wanted Cousy. And Cousy wanted to get into that game so bad he could taste it.

"He's *got* to put me in now," I thought. "He's *got* to!"

Now my name was all over the place. That "COUSY!" came bouncing off the walls and echoing down from the ceiling. You couldn't hear anything else.

I looked over toward Doggie. He was crouched near the sideline, his eyes glued to the action in front of him. Then somebody on our club called a time out. Doggie straightened up and turned towards me. He yelled something and beckoned in my direction. I was on my feet before he had finished the gesture, heading towards the scorer's table to report. As I ran by Doggie, he cupped his hands and yelled for me to replace McMullen.

The next five minutes must have been the most confused of my life. I don't recall much of anything that happened except that I kept reaching for the ball like a drowning man. I couldn't get my hands on it fast enough, couldn't get it into the basket fast enough, couldn't do anything fast enough.

I guess I was trying to do in five minutes all the things I hadn't been given a chance to do in the previous forty-three. And I pretty nearly succeeded. I took seven shots at the basket in the last four and a half minutes and hit with six of them. Those twelve points won the ball game for us.

○

When the final buzzer sounded, I turned and rushed for the locker room, obsessed with an absurd desire to shower and get out of there before Doggie saw me. I was hysterical, partly from anger and partly from sheer relief. And as I stripped off my suit in front of the locker, I was crying like a baby.

I remember Father Tiernan coming over to try to calm me down, and I have a vague recollection of guys shaking hands with me and pounding me on the back. And maybe Doggie

shook hands with me too. He always went around shaking
hands with each man after every ball game anyhow.

Finally I got under the shower and stayed there a long time.
When I came out, I was calmer, but I didn't want to talk to
anyone. I dressed and headed for the team bus. And as we
rode back to Worcester, I sat staring at the lights as they
flashed by on the turnpike, and I talked to nobody.

I played through the rest of the season and the N.C.A.A.
tournament without exchanging a word with Doggie. The
only time he spoke to me was when he put me back into a
game after taking me out for a rest. But if he held anything
against me, he didn't show it in the way he handled me on
the court. I was on his first five, and he started me in every
game.

We were the defending N.C.A.A. champions, and we started
the tournament as if we were going all the way. We got by the
first round without any trouble, beating Michigan in a walk.
I had one of my biggest nights in Madison Square Garden,
scoring twenty-three points.

But the next night I had my worst. Against Kentucky, which
eventually won the title, I missed thirteen out of fourteen shots
I took at the basket, and we got murdered. It took me years to
live down that game.

That was the end of the season for us. We dragged ourselves back to Worcester and broke up for the year. And still
Doggie and I didn't speak.

One day, several weeks later, I was fooling around in the
gym by myself when Doggie walked in. He watched me for a
few minutes, then called me over.

When we stood face to face, he said, "I'd like to talk to you
for a couple of minutes."

I was glad.

"Sure," I said.

"Cooz," he said, "I've just accepted an offer to coach the Boston Celtics next year."

I took a long breath.

"I want you to know that I'm sorry for anything that might have prevented us from getting along better," he said. "It's too bad that there seems to have been a personality clash between us, but now I'd like to shake hands and part friends."

He held out his hand, and I took it.

"That's fine with me, Doggie," I said. "I know there was never anything personal involved, and I guess I did plenty of things I shouldn't have done. I'm sorry about those. But it's all over now."

We looked at each other a minute.

Then I said, "Best of luck with the Celtics, Doggie."

"Thanks," he said.

Then he walked out.

Years later, in March of 1956, a banquet was given in my honor at the Hotel Sheraton in Worcester. Doggie was coaching at Dartmouth and had been invited to attend. He was sick and couldn't make it, but here is the wire he sent:

A strep infection prevents my joining you in lauding Bob Cousy, basketball's greatest. His contribution to basketball is not only superb play but inspiration to youngsters everywhere who aspire to his heights. His basketball success belongs to Bob himself, his development into a fine man to Holy Cross College. Best wishes to you all.

That wire is one of my proudest possessions.

CHAPTER 9 | *Shop talk*

WHILE I WASN'T CRAZY ABOUT DOGGIE JULIAN, I ALWAYS respected him as a great coach. He taught me a lot of basketball. Morty Arkin gave me the fundamentals of the game when I fooled around O'Connell playground as a kid. Lew Grummond, stiff-necked, strict and conservative, showed me what teamwork means. But Doggie not only combined the two but taught me the basic plays which helped me take advantage of every possible asset nature had given me. Grummond: "Do as I say, and don't change." Julian: "Here's the frame. You supply the picture."

Both were sound basketball men, but while Grummond always played it straight, Doggie left the door open for anything. His system was fresh, smart, "give-and-go." You could move around all you wanted with his formations and take advantage of opportunities any way you liked. Grummond wouldn't let you do that. You followed a set pattern with him, and heaven help you if you did anything on your own. I've seen kids bawled out by Grummond for scoring baskets because they didn't do it his way. With Doggie a basket was a basket.

Doggie's wide open game was designed for the material at hand, and that was probably the basic difference between him and Lew Grummond. Grummond had his own system, and he had to have certain types of players. He was always looking for those players so that he could suit them to his system. But Julian did it the other way around. He took the players he had and gave them the system best suited to them. And because he did things that way he was, on the basketball court at least, my type of coach. It was too bad we couldn't get along better.

Doggie's basic formation was the figure eight, a constantly moving weave which permitted everyone or anyone to handle the ball. It's a beautiful thing to watch when done correctly, particularly from up above. I've always felt that the place to watch a basketball game is a balcony rather than the floor because then you can see what a well-drilled team is doing by the pattern it forms. In the figure eight the ball is always in motion and so is the team that's handling it. Someone is always getting into position to take a pass, and as you watch from above, you can see the way men are moving. From the floor it appears that they are coming out of nowhere, but every step is in accordance with a preconceived pattern.

There are dozens of options, depending on what the defensive team is doing. If the defense is too tight, your team can switch from one side or the other. Sometimes it's better to continue the weave in exactly the same pattern with one man after another coming out from the figure eight. Something has to give sooner or later, but it's one good way to set up a shot, particularly if the game is close and the final buzzer is only seconds away. Then that one shot can mean the ball game. But if you lose the ball, you can't take the shot, so the figure eight helps a team hang on for the shot.

When a team of good ball-handlers is using the figure eight, it's pretty hard to steal the ball. I've seen teams go frantic trying to get possession in the dying seconds. Usually, some-body would get fouled under those conditions so we'd get a free shot anyway. And with college rules as they were when I was at Holy Cross, deliberate fouls paid off if a team was more than a point ahead. It was always worth while to give up a possible point in return for a few precious seconds and possession of the ball if the foul was sunk.

The figure eight was a classic example of give-and-go basket-ball, which requires speed and clever ball-handling. The system is especially effective if you don't have an outstandingly big guy, which we didn't. With a man six feet, eight or nine inches tall, you play a pivot offense—in other words, he stays in the pivot, and the others feed him the ball. If he's having a good night, you score in buckets; if he isn't, you may as well go home. But with give-and-go, where everyone is given an equal chance to score, you don't have to worry if one man isn't hit-ting. There's always somebody else who is.

Julian platooned us during my freshman year. I usually played with Bob McMullen, Andy Laska, Frank Oftring and a fifth man, normally George Kaftan, drawn from the first five. All five of us could handle the ball well, and Kaftan was a great shooter. When we started showing flashes that sports writers claimed were something like genius, everyone began calling us the Fancy Pants A.C.

The figure eight, wide open as it was, gave us all a great chance to operate the trick stuff that made the Holy Cross team of the late forties one of the most colorful college out-fits in the country. We fooled around with behind-the-back and

over-the-shoulder passes and such gags as looking one way
and passing the other. This stuff was my specialty.

They weren't gags for us, although people got a big kick
out of them. I learned to pass accurately behind my back in
high school, but I only did it when I couldn't pass any other
way. Once in a great while I pulled a stunt for the hell of it
but only when we were so far ahead that the game was getting
dull. Normally I saved the trick stuff for the time when I
might need it.

It was exactly such an emergency that started me on one of
my best known maneuvers—my shift from one hand to the
other behind my back. It happened in a game with Loyola
during my junior year at Holy Cross. Loyola had a great
club that year, and so did we. The Boston Garden was sold
out. The game was a real seat-squirmer, with first one team
and then the other moving into the lead. We finally got down
to the last minute with the game so close that a basket would
settle it.

We got the ball and called time out. We huddled and decided to hold it for one shot, which I would take. Then we
passed the ball around on our figure eight, waiting for the
big break. Finally, with about eight seconds to go, it was
time for some action. This time when I got the ball, I didn't
pass it to anyone but started driving for the basket.

I was on the left side of the court, driving to my right. My
opponent had been overplaying me to the right all night, and
this time, as I got down close to the right of the basket, there
he was, well on my right, boxing me in so that I couldn't shoot
at all. Time was running out, and I had to score that basket.
When I saw how tightly this guy was playing me, I tried to
shift hands, but he was right on top of me.

There was only one thing left: to shift hands behind my

back if I could. I'd never tried it, but I had no choice. So without changing direction, I bounced the ball behind my back with my right hand and picked it up with my left, then drove in and dunked the winning basket into the hoop with a left-handed hook shot.

The whole place went nuts and so did I. But from that night on I was branded. Every time we were in a tight game the crowd expected me to bail us out with some miracle shot. I was never able to convince people that I can't do this sort of thing whenever I want. I've got to have the right spot.

I can pull this stunt from time to time because I've got a funny build. I'm not tall for a basketball player—about six feet, one and a half inches. I'm not particularly heavy. My playing weight is about 175. I'm not awfully fast. There are dozens of players in the pro league who can outrun me in a race the length of the court. I look puny in a basketball game. People who see me for the first time think I'm unfed and untended. Sometimes they feel sorry for me.

But I've got my points. I have unusually long arms and sharply sloping ape-like shoulders. And if you've ever noticed an ape, his arms are so long that he can easily clasp them behind his back. So can I.

I have huge, ham-like hands. My fingers are long and strong, and I can grip a basketball like a baseball. I have tremendously powerful thighs, which give me the strength to run all night. My muscles are resilient, and I can stop and change direction quickly. And I have unusual peripheral vision. I can see more than most people out of the corners of my eyes. I don't have to turn my head to find out what's going on at either side. It sometimes appears that I'm throwing the ball without looking. I'm looking all right but out of the corners of my eyes.

When I was at Holy Cross, people used to oh and ah when

I passed the ball over my shoulder like a quarterback using the statue-of-liberty play. He stands as if to pass, and a guy comes around behind him, takes the ball out of his hands and runs. The over-the-shoulder pass is also dependent on a smart receiver. All I had to do was stand still and act as though I were going to shoot or pass. Instead, I'd simply drop the ball behind me and pray that the receiver was there to take it. If he wasn't, I'd look pretty silly.

Unlike the behind-the-back shift, which I used on the spur of a desperate moment, this over-the-shoulder pass was a planned operation. It's used today by many good ball-handlers. Practically all the pro teams use it. When I was in college I pulled it with Andy Laska and George Kaftan.

These stunts are great when they work and when they're necessary, but they're highly inadvisable if there's no reason for them. Nobody likes to be made to look stupid, and a trick can make an opponent look very stupid indeed. Get him mad, and you run a fine chance of seeing him run wild. He won't mind the stunt if he knows it's the only way you can keep control of the ball. But he'll be red-eyed if you do it just to show off.

When Nat (Sweetwater) Clifton first joined the New York Knickerbockers, he came directly from the Harlem Globe-trotters, an independent team famous for its clowning and great ball-handling. Clifton, who has tremendous hands, had a hatful of tricks, one of which was to stretch his arms way out while gripping the ball, then instead of throwing it or shooting, bringing it back, still holding the ball. It killed the customers and was very funny when pulled with the Globe-trotters. But he tried it against us for laughs. He got the laughs from the crowd but not from the Celtics.

When I got the ball and happened to be near Sweetwater, I let it run up one arm and down the other, keeping control of it all the time. It wasn't one of my favorite moves because I'm never sure it will work, but it worked that time, and from then on Sweetwater played us straight.

○

College basketball was a pretty serious business with me, but I had my share of laughs. I think the funniest thing I ever saw on a basketball court happened while I was playing for Holy Cross. We had a game against St. Anselm's with a Worcester referee working. About halfway through it, he called me on a foul.

Now anyone who has seen a basketball game knows that the referee is always the villain when he calls a foul, and the player he calls it on is always the innocent victim. There isn't a basketball player alive who doesn't register anything from simple annoyance to wild-eyed rage when a foul is called on him, even if it's a palpable foul and one that he knows he's committed. At the very least, he'll wear a pained expression. He won't necessarily be mad at the referee; he's more likely to be sore at himself. But no matter who the object of his beef may be, he'll always turn toward the referee first. Like the baseball player, a hoopster knows his protest won't do any good, but he'll kick on general principles anyway.

When the foul was called on me in the St. Anselm's game, I automatically turned towards the referee to squawk. But when I spun around to argue, I couldn't get a word out of my mouth. The referee was trying to blow his whistle, give the foul signal and yell to the bench, but he couldn't do anything. He was too busy trying to stuff his false teeth back in his mouth.

It broke me up, and it still does when I think about it.

One day when I was around the athletic office, one of the

assistants said, "Hey, Cooz, we need a guy to sell tickets. How about giving us a hand?"

"Sure," I said.

As I moved in behind a cage, he remarked, "You probably won't sell many. These guys will all recognize you."

But the first customer bought a ticket without saying anything and so did the second. There was a line of maybe twenty-five or thirty guys. As one after the other moved up to the window, paid his money, got his ticket and moved away, I began to get mildly upset. I thought they'd all recognize me. None of them did.

But the minute I walked out from behind that cage, one guy after another stopped me.

"It only goes to prove," somebody said, "that people never look twice at ticket-sellers of the male gender."

○

I was, of course, delighted when Doggie Julian left Holy Cross to coach the Celtics. And when Lester (Buster) Sheary was announced as his successor, I was even happier. Sheary was appointed by the college, but he was selected by the players. I think that may have been the only occasion in modern times when that's happened in big-time college coaching.

Sheary was and still is assistant athletic director for the city of Worcester, although he doesn't coach Holy Cross basketball any more. He was Julian's chief scout, and he coached us during the fall when Doggie was busy with his football duties. We all knew Buster well.

He was a very wonderful guy. Although he was not tall, he was stocky and heavy-set and gave the impression of great strength. He had china-blue eyes that could look right through you. When Buster was mad, you wanted to get down on your knees and apologize. He was a born leader. He could talk to you for two minutes, and you'd be all fired up for an entire game.

He was one of the toughest guys I ever knew. I've seen him emphasize a point by smashing his fist against a brick wall until the knuckles bled. He could give a locker-room fight talk that would have done justice to Knute Rockne. Buster was, I imagine, much like Rockne. He had that indefinable something which could inspire a whole team.

He earned the name Buster when he played fullback on the Catholic University football team. He could tear an opposing line apart. Nothing bothered him. And he coached like he must have played, battling for every point. He hated like the devil to lose.

"Always remember," he said one day, "if you don't want a thing to hurt you, it won't. And if nothing can hurt you, how can anything beat you?"

Of course, we all knew Buster was tough, but we also knew he was very fair. He never played favorites and never could. He never let his personal feelings about a ballplayer influence his judgment. Buster ran a basketball team the way a pilot runs an airplane. Every man was a cog in a machine.

At the time Julian resigned we didn't have a single senior on the Holy Cross basketball team. That meant every one of us would be back the following year. As soon as we heard that Doggie was leaving, Frank Oftring and I got up a petition asking for Sheary, and circulated it among the boys on the team. After everyone signed it, we turned it over to Father Tiernan, the athletic moderator, and Gene Flynn, the director of athletics. Later Father Tiernan told me, "We were going to hire Buster anyway, and we were delighted that you fellows wanted him so badly."

We had two great seasons with Buster, although we missed winning any titles. During my senior year, the 1949-50 season, we had a winning streak of twenty-six straight games. I couldn't believe we'd go all the way, but I was just beginning to get some vague hopes when we were stopped by Columbia. They beat us in their own gym in New York. People said later the gym licked us because it was small and, of course, strange to us. That was so much malarkey. We were defying the law of averages by then, and somebody had to beat us. If it hadn't been Columbia, it would have been someone else.

North Carolina State knocked us out of the N.C.A.A. tournament that year. We all wanted to win it for Buster. I never felt that way about a guy before, and I was very much upset when we got eliminated.

But bad as I felt at the N.C.A.A. tournament, I felt worse at the Sugar Bowl tournament a few weeks earlier in New Orleans, and it wasn't because of a basketball loss. Without meaning it, I was instrumental in hurting Sheary.

Buster was one of the most naïve men I ever knew. He was strictly on the level and believed that everyone was on the level with him. He was fiercely proud of us and certain that none of us would ever do anything to make him feel otherwise. Among other things, Buster was a nut on smoking and drinking. He couldn't imagine us indulging in either vice, which he felt was as bad as larceny or maybe even murder.

Actually, we were all good for an occasional bottle of beer after a tough ball game. Sometimes we'd even have two, although I didn't go for more than that. But a little beer relaxed me, and I still like to take it when the going's been rough.

We got beaten in the Sugar Bowl tournament by St. Louis

University, which then had a team revolving around Ed Macauley, later a Celtics teammate and close friend of mine. We were all down in the dumps after the game, and we went out for a couple of beers while Buster apparently went to his room and moped. The next day Bob Curran, Sheary's assistant coach, came over to me and said, "Buster wants to see you and Kaftan in his room."

When George and I went up to see him, Sheary was obviously upset about something more than the loss of the ball game. As we walked in, I could see he was clenching his fists in an effort to keep control of himself. He looked at us a minute or two, then in a cracked voice he said, "I hear you fellows went out and had a couple of drinks after the game last night. How could you do this to me?"

"But Buster," I said, "we just had a couple of beers to relax."

He stared hard at me, tears welling up in his eyes.

"So it's true! I thought I could trust you."

Then he turned away, muttering over and over, "How could you do this? Nobody ever did this to me before."

Suddenly he walked over to Kaftan. His fists were clenched again, and for a minute I thought he was going to throw a punch. But just as suddenly he caught hold of himself. Squaring his shoulders, he barked, "Get out! Quick!"

George got out. Sheary, still fighting tears, looked back at me, and I felt so badly I nearly busted out crying myself. I didn't have the heart to tell him the whole team drank beer after the game. If he knew that, he would have flipped. So when he asked me if anyone else had been with us, I told him, "No." As far as I know, Buster still thinks that Kaftan and I were the only ones who had any beer that night. But I couldn't pacify him, and it wasn't until the next day that he was himself again.

Buster always put the boys ahead of everything else. He fought for us regardless of the circumstances. When we went to the N.C.A.A. tournament in my senior year, Sheary battled with the athletic office until the school agreed to take fourteen men instead of twelve, the usual number. He didn't need the extra two men—he just wanted them to have the trip. He also fought for a sports public relations director and got the school to hire one. And it was only at Buster's insistence that the college provided private limousines instead of buses for comfort on short trips.

While Kaftan and I made a good combination on the basketball floor, there was no real feeling of companionship between us. We were utterly different in almost every conceivable way. George always went around with a big smile on his face, and he made a tremendous impression on strangers. A big, handsome, dark-haired guy, he was a personality kid. I was anything but. In college I was very quiet, very reserved and very shy. Kaftan and I didn't pal around together; we were thrown together.

I'll never forget his last words to me on a college basketball court. We were playing Springfield, and Kaftan was graduating at mid-term. This was his final game. There was less than a minute to go, and we were way ahead. I got the ball and drove in with Kaftan behind me. This was an option play, and I had my choice of feeding him the ball over my shoulder or scoring myself. This time I went in and shot the basket.

"For the love of Mike," Kaftan said, "don't you ever pass?" Those were his parting words to me.

IO | *The fixers*

ONE NIGHT DURING MY JUNIOR YEAR AT HOLY CROSS, WE WENT to New Haven to play Yale. An acquaintance of mine from New York came up for the game. He was a fellow who called me for tickets occasionally. This wasn't unusual. A good many guys called me for tickets, particularly when we played in Madison Square Garden. Except for my folks and very close friends, I never tried to get free ducats. But sometimes it was even hard to get tickets to buy.

In any event, I told this guy to meet me in the lobby of the New Haven Auditorium, where the sellout game was being played. I got there right after dinner, and since I needed a little exercise, I suggested that we take a walk around the block. We talked about basketball in general and passed the time of day for half an hour or so. Then we stopped on the sidewalk across the street from the entrance to the Auditorium, and I handed him his tickets. He paid me, and I put the money in my wallet. Then I shook hands with him, walked across the street and headed for the dressing room.

I promptly forgot the incident, which meant nothing to

me. I wouldn't have recalled it to this day if it hadn't been brought to my attention. That happened four years later, under most unpleasant circumstances, in the district attorney's office in New York City. The New Haven incident turned out to be the prime basis for widespread stories that I was involved in the college basketball betting scandals, which were exposed in 1951.

If college basketball could live through that nightmare, it could live through anything. One minute the college game was the biggest thing on the winter sports circuit; the next, it was in absolute disgrace, completely discredited and unhappily standing by while its dirty linen was being washed in public.

No one really knows what happened or what caused the scandals. There isn't much question, however, that the game became so big in New York that it got completely out of hand. During the years that I was at Holy Cross, it had branched out from the local gyms to the big city arenas. To my mind, there's nothing wrong with that if the local gyms remain in use. It seems to me that half a dozen games a year in a big arena makes perfectly good sense. But the New York City colleges were playing almost all their games in Madison Square Garden—when they could get the place. Only Columbia remained on its campus, but the other schools in New York were fighting for games in the Garden.

The Garden buildup was so terrific that after a while almost any college basketball doubleheader was an automatic sellout. All the colleges involved would collect huge checks. When top teams were playing, it was nearly impossible to buy tickets.

Any time a sport becomes that big it attracts gamblers. It's impossible to control betting on any sport; the idea is to protect the players from direct contact with gamblers who might be plotting a fix. Ever since the Chicago Black Sox baseball scandal of 1919, gamblers have been kept away from athletes. But in the late forties somebody slipped up, and college kids who had never done a dishonest thing in their lives were trapped.

One trouble was this mania for playing games in Madison Square Garden, where gamblers have been congregating for years. It was too easy for spectators to approach athletes there. No attempt was made to protect the athletes from the public. In nine hundred ninety-nine cases out of one thousand, they don't need protection. But because of that one-in-a-thousandth case, they must have it. Promoters realize that today. But in the late forties, everyone got careless. Gamblers were approaching ballplayers with propositions, and to some kids the propositions sounded too good to turn down.

As it happens, basketball easily lends itself to heavy gambling because today it's a game of big scores. After World War II ended, the tight games, such as we used to play when I was in high school, went out the window. Everyone was playing a wide-open game. Nobody worried about how many points the other team collected; the big thing was to get more points yourself.

With all this heavy concentration on scoring, the gamblers figured out new ways of paying off. The most popular was to place bets on the "point spread" rather than on the final score. In this way, gamblers could get all the action they wanted on any game, even if one team were a huge favorite over the other. Instead of betting on the winner, they could bet on the margin of victory.

For example, a team might be designated as a twelve-point favorite. If it won by more than that, its backers collected; if it didn't, they lost. Since it wasn't necessary to lose a game for the gamblers to collect, the fixers had an argument when they approached players. In most cases, they didn't ask a boy to lose. All they asked was that he arrange for his team to win by a margin less than the point spread. This was called "shaving points."

The New York newspapers made a big fuss over the point spread, and that didn't help the situation. At least one paper led its sports section with point spread information almost every day. Thus the boys involved with the fixers couldn't help but realize that they were in the middle of a very big deal. And, of course, it made gambling easy. In other sports the gamblers had to go to elaborate lengths to find out the odds on any event. But all they had to do before the basketball scandals broke was look in the newspapers.

The point spread got more attention than the outcome of the game. After a while nobody seemed to care who won or lost; the only thing that counted was the margin of victory. Naturally, the players weren't blind to the swelling importance of the point spread. But most of them didn't really care. Their only interest was in winning the game.

When I was at Holy Cross, we had no interest whatever in such things as point spreads. It never occurred to me—or to the other guys on the team either, as far as I know—that gamblers were actually reaching kids on any of the teams. None of us ever worried about the gambling part. We were so wrapped up in our own ball club that all we thought about was winning games. Never in our wildest dreams did any of us think that guys on other clubs had a financial interest in the point spread.

The scandals broke like the folds of an accordion. District Attorney Frank S. Hogan of New York announced arrests piecemeal so that instead of coming out all at once, the story leaked out gradually. As a result, the scandals were headline news for months. Almost every week some big-name college basketball player confessed to doing business with gamblers. Sometimes one would admit having thrown a game, but in most cases it was simply a matter of shaving points.

Who can call a boy a criminal for doing that? A $500 offer to keep down a winning score is a pretty strong inducement. College kids on sports scholarships don't have that kind of money to spend. Most of them are beating their brains out trying to make enough on the side for spending money. When a boy can collect five hundred bucks without purposely losing a game, he's got to have a pretty strong will to turn the money down.

Friends of mine, boys whom I played against in high school, were involved in this thing. I agree they did wrong; there's no question about that. But they were all branded for life as cheaters, and some even went to jail. As I look back today, after seven years of professional basketball, I feel more strongly than ever that the punishments hardly fitted the crimes. I've been burned in business deals, and I hear of others being hurt even worse by guys indulging in sharp practices. These characters live on the edge of the law, yet get away with far worse than anything a college boy could do, on or off a basketball court. To me a grown man who cheats should have the book thrown at him. But an impressionable college kid with no spare money in his pocket and a clean record behind him should certainly be given a second chance.

When I was going to college, five dollars looked like a lot of money. The same was true of most of the athletes who went to college with me. I think it would have been a terrific temptation if some sharpie had come up to me and said, "Instead of winning by fifteen points tonight, win by ten, and I'll give you $500."

Ed Macauley, who was with me on the Celtics at the time

the scandals broke, put it all in a nutshell when he said, "If anyone had ever approached me to shave points when I was in college, I wouldn't have given it a second thought. I would have turned him down cold and told him to peddle his papers somewhere else and leave me alone. Maybe I'd have taken a poke at him."

Then after a pause, he added, "I didn't have a dime in those days. I'm sure glad no one approached me."

Before the investigations were over, it was announced that the New York district attorney's office had uncovered forty-nine fixed games in twenty-three cities and seventeen states. In 1951 alone, Hogan made over thirty arrests, and there were more in the years immediately following.

I guess they must have checked every college that had a top basketball team during the years I was in school. I don't know when they started or when they finished, but they covered Holy Cross with a fine-toothed comb. I not only assumed that they would ask about me, friends told me they did. And somewhere along the line, rumors sprang up that I was involved in the scandals and was on the verge of being picked up as a fixer.

I would have had to be blind and deaf not to be aware of these rumors. Every major college player of that period was considered a suspect, I suppose. So many top stars, several of them All-American players, confessed to throwing games or shaving points that after a while people began thinking that *every* college stand-out must have been in on the deal. At one point a national sports magazine refused to plan any basketball stories because the editors were afraid that the subject would be disclosed as a point shaver before a piece about him got into print.

I joined the Boston Celtics in the fall of 1950, and the first news break on the scandals came the following January. For the next couple of years it was touch and go. Guys whom nobody dreamed were involved suddenly confessed. Some had already graduated and were playing professional ball. One entire team in the pro league, the Indianapolis Olympians, was wrecked by the scandals.

"Who's next?" That was the big question in those days. Naturally we Celtics talked about the situation. We were all ready to swear by one another, and in fact, not one of us was involved. But the rumors kept cropping up, and fair or unfair, you can't stop rumors overnight. I was a college star in the late forties; many college stars in the late forties were fixers; therefore, went the logic, I was a fixer.

But until early 1953 the rumors about me were as vague as they were vicious. Then something happened that made them more concrete. One night in January or February as I was walking out of Madison Square Garden in New York after a Celtics game, two guys stopped me. They were just ordinary-looking guys, dressed in street clothes, very polite and almost apologetic.

"Bob Cousy?" one asked.

I nodded.

"Sorry to bother you," he said. "We're detectives. We'd like to ask you a few questions. Would you be willing to come to the district attorney's office and help us out?"

I didn't feel like jumping over the fence and running, but I won't deny I had a funny sensation. Guilty or innocent, anyone asked a question like that would get a queer flutter in his stomach for a minute. But I had nothing to hide.

"I can't this trip," I said. "We're leaving town right away. But we'll be back in ten days or so. Will that be okay?"

"Fine," the detective said. "And thanks a lot."

Then the two walked away.

The more I thought about it, the less worried I was. It figured that they'd want to quiz everybody, and I was no exception. But there were people walking by when these guys talked to me. They might have been recognized by newspapermen. Nobody was printing the story, but anyone who did know these guys could jump to some quick conclusions. And nothing travels faster than an ugly rumor.

"Two detectives talked to Cousy in the Garden!" I could almost hear the whispers. And when I had a chance to think straight, I realized that the reporters covering the district attorney's office probably knew I'd be called before I did. Whatever the situation, the smart guys were already circulating the word, "Cousy's next! Cousy's next!"

Back in Boston Walter Brown, the owner of the Celtics, called me into his office and said, "Bob, tell me the truth. Is there anything to these rumors that are going around?"

I looked him squarely in the eyes and said, "Walter, I have never done a dishonest thing on or off the basketball court."

He breathed a long sigh.

"That's good enough for me," he said.

"I've been asked to appear in the district attorney's office," I told him. "They've got some questions they want me to answer. I told them I'd see them our next trip to New York."

"Good," he said. "I know you'll tell them the truth. And remember, Bob, I'm with you all the way."

Later Brown told me that up to the time I assured him I wasn't involved in the scandals nothing had ever worried him as much as those rumors. I couldn't blame him. He had already spent nearly eight years and thousands of dollars trying to build up professional basketball in Boston. His Celtics revolved around Macauley, Bill Sharman and me. If I had been mixed up with the gamblers, Walter was convinced that the Celtics would have gone right down the drain.

I reported at the office of Vincent O'Connor, New York district attorney, early one afternoon in mid-February of 1953. I sat around for two or three hours before they called me in, and when I got into the office, I was surrounded by five or six of O'Connor's men. Before I realized what was happening, O'Connor had launched into a lengthy accusation.

He was sure I'd been involved with the gamblers when I was at Holy Cross. He told me I had been implicated by a bookmaker who had died the previous summer. This bookmaker had given the names of several college basketball players with whom he said he was doing business.

"Your name is on that list," O'Connor said, "so you might as well tell us about it."

"I don't know the guy," I said. "I've never even heard of him."

"Now, come on," a detective insisted, "you can't expect us to believe that."

That set the tone of the next few hours, the most uncomfortable I've ever spent in my life. The district attorney and his boys threw questions at me from all angles, and I sat in the middle and tried to answer them. But nobody believed me. The more they asked and the more I answered, the less convinced they seemed to be. We were getting nowhere fast.

As the hours went by and I realized I wasn't making any impression whatever, I started to get discouraged. I didn't panic, and I don't really think I was frightened. But I had told these men everything I knew—which was nothing—and still they came back with the same question or ones designed to trap me.

I had only one thing going for me: I was telling the truth. I didn't care what that dead bookmaker had told them. He'd been lying if he'd put my name on his list, and I knew it. But trying to convince the district attorney and his men of that fact was something else again. They simply wouldn't believe me.

Finally, one of the detectives looked at his watch and said, "It's getting late. I'm going out to dinner. How about joining me, Bob?"

"I'd be delighted," I said, and I was. Anything was better than staying in that room.

We indulged in nothing more strenuous than small talk, and during the meal I had a chance to think a little. I came to the conclusion that I had been crazy to walk into the district attorney's office without a lawyer. So when we got back to the courthouse, I said to the detective, "Look, I've shown my good will coming down here without counsel. I'd like to call a lawyer before I go back in there. Is it all right if I do?"

"I'll check with the boss and let you know," he replied. "You wait here."

It was about seven o'clock in the evening. The detective disappeared in O'Connor's office, and I sat down in the anteroom. I didn't see him or anyone else for four hours. And as the minutes ticked by, I didn't know which was worse—having all those guys in there throw questions at me until I was dizzy or waiting outside alone, wondering what was coming next.

I figured the strategy was to wear me down by keeping me waiting, but instead of wearing me down, the wait irritated me. The longer I sat there, the madder I got. When a detective finally came out, I jumped up and started, "What the—!"

He stopped me before I got out more than a couple of words. "Calm down," he said. "Everything's under control. We've got a few things to tell you, then we'll have one more question to ask you. After that, you can go."

"You mean you're not going to want me around any more?"

The guy just smiled and told me to follow him. In the office O'Connor brought me up-to-date.

One of the things they had asked me about during their afternoon quiz period was what I knew about two men five or six years older than I. I knew both of them and said so. I added that this was the first time I'd heard their names in connection with the basketball scandals.

It turned out that while I was having dinner with the detective, the district attorney had called them both in. And during the four hours I was sweating out in the anteroom, they were answering questions. Finally both confessed and cleared me completely.

What had happened was this:

The boys had been doing business with the dead bookie, but they were double-crossing him, playing both ends against the middle. In my case, they told the bookie they knew me, which was true. But they also told him that they thought they could get me to cooperate by shaving points in certain Holy Cross games. They may have thought so, but they never tried to prove it. Neither had approached me on the subject. The only times I ever heard from either was when they wanted tickets to a basketball game.

These guys kept the bookie on the string for a year and a half. Every time there was a Holy Cross game in which the bookie was interested, they collected money from him, ostensibly for me but actually for themselves. And, of course, they were also collecting their own fee from the bookie.

They had a nice little racket going as long as the bookie was satisfied. But the bookie got suspicious when the Holy Cross games that were supposed to be fixed didn't come out right. Out of six games they said they'd arranged with me, five went the other way, and the bookie lost his shirt.

Finally, the bookie accused the boys of double-crossing him. They not only protested their innocence but offered to prove that I was the one double-crossing him, not they. One of them told the bookie that he was going to give me some money in a week or so for shaving points in a Holy Cross-Yale game at New Haven. Furthermore, he said he'd do it within sight of the bookie.

So the following week, this guy and the bookie went to New Haven together. That was the day I met the man to give him the tickets he'd asked me for. When we walked around the block, the bookie walked behind us. And when I gave him the tickets and he paid me for them, the bookie was standing across the street watching us. That was enough for the bookie. He was convinced that the boys were all right and I was a louse. And when he submitted his list of basketball players to the district attorney's office, he was delighted to include me.

As I sat listening to the story, I got a wonderful warm feeling of absolute relief. Obviously these fellows finally did believe me. And when they were through telling me the story of my "friends," they asked me that one question: did I remember having received money from one of these men before a game in New Haven?

With that much of a memory jog, I certainly did. The whole incident in front of the Auditorium came back. I explained it in great detail, and when I had finished, a detective said, "That's fine. We're satisfied that you're in the clear. As a matter of fact, the man already told us that story."

I was so relieved I forgot I had gone back into that office mad, forgot that I had wanted a lawyer, forgot everything except that these wonderful guys believed my story. When the district attorney asked me if I would be willing to repeat it before the grand jury, I readily agreed. And several months later I did.

At that time O'Connor thanked me for my cooperation and assured me he would be glad to provide proof of my innocence if I ever needed it. This, of course, meant everything to me. By then I was a partner in a boys' camp, and I had to avoid the least suspicion of evil.

○

Rotten as the scandals were, one good thing came out of them. It is the consensus of most people who know—and I agree—that professional basketball didn't start to flourish until after the scandals hit. Up to that time the pro game was struggling. But when people temporarily lost faith in the college game, they turned their attention to the pros, who have since been doing better every year.

I suppose there are people who think the pros can be reached the way the college boys were. But anyone with a grain of intelligence must realize how ridiculous this is. In the college game there was almost always one outstanding star. The fixer who reached him reached the team. But every professional basketball team is made up of ten All-America players. No one man can control the score. In order to fix a game, a gambler would have to reach nearly all ten men, and even if he could get them to cooperate, the price would be too high to make it worth his while.

I don't believe any pro basketball player would be idiotic enough to do business with a fixer, even if he were so inclined. The average salary in our league is about $8,500, and with extras like playoff games it can run higher. Most players are family men. Practically all have outside businesses, the success of which depends on personal reputations. A man's good name is the most precious thing he owns. A pro basket-ball player's good name is also worth money in dollars and cents. It would be insane to drop all this down the drain for the few illicit bucks a fixer would pay off.

| CHAPTER | 11 | *Fast, loose and always* |

I BECAME SO WRAPPED UP IN BASKETBALL THROUGHOUT school and college that it seemed as though nothing else mattered. Well, not quite. At Holy Cross I maintained a high scholastic average—in the nineties my junior and senior years —and after a slow start late in my junior year at high school, I began to get seriously interested in girls. At first it was strictly a matter of taking a girl home from a dance or going to a movie or something like that. Even the girl whose name I took when I played in the Long Island Press League, Joan Kilduff, was little more than a casual friend. We had a crush on each other but weren't serious. But somewhere in the early part of my senior year at Andrew Jackson I became aware of the existence of Marie Ritterbusch, whom everyone called "Missie."

She went to Bishop McDonald, a girls' parochial school in Brooklyn. Her brother, Ed, was in the gang of older guys who used to play basketball around O'Connell playground when I was a kid. Missie herself went with an older crowd.

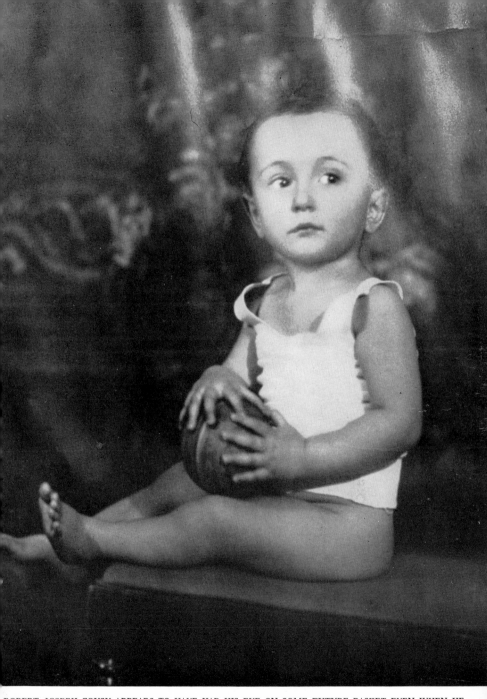

ROBERT JOSEPH COUSY APPEARS TO HAVE HAD HIS EYE ON SOME FUTURE BASKET EVEN WHEN HE WAS STILL PUSHING ONE YEAR OLD. AND IS THAT A BASKETBALL HE HOLDS IN HIS HANDS? "MY MOTHER STILL LIKES TO TELL PEOPLE THAT IT IS A BASKETBALL AND THAT THE PICTURE PROVES I WAS EARMARKED FOR BASKETBALL LONG BEFORE ANY OF US HEARD OF THE GAME."

(ABOVE, LEFT) BOB IS PICTURED WITH HIS MOTHER, MRS. JOSEPH COUSY, ON THE OCCASION OF HIS GRADUATION FROM ANDREW JACKSON HIGH SCHOOL, LONG ISLAND, IN 1945. (ABOVE, RIGHT) YOUNG COUSY, HIS DAD AND A FRIEND OF THE FAMILY ENJOY THE WARM SUN OF THE CATSKILLS DURING A SUMMER VACATION. ALTHOUGH HIS DAD IS AN ARDENT COUSY FAN, HIS MOTHER STILL WORRIES ABOUT POSSIBLE INJURIES TO HER SON. (BELOW) BOB—SECOND FROM RIGHT—POSES WITH FOUR EAST SIDE PALS. DESPITE THE INCONVENIENCES OF LIFE IN A TENEMENT DISTRICT, "I HAD A WHALE OF A GOOD TIME PLAYING STICKBALL AND STOOPBALL AND BOXBALL AND ROASTING MICKEYS IN TIN CANS AND SWIMMING RAW AMONG THE COAL AND GARBAGE BARGES ON THE EAST RIVER."

BOB WAS THE MOST FAMOUS CITIZEN IN ST. ALBANS, LONG ISLAND, THE DAY HE WAS NAMED
CAPTAIN OF NEW YORK CITY'S ALL-SCHOLASTIC TEAM, WHICH INCLUDED THE FIVE BOROUGHS OF
THE METROPOLIS. FROM LEFT TO RIGHT (ABOVE, LEFT) ARE COUSY, REPRESENTING ANDREW
JACKSON H.S.; GEORGE FEIGENBAUM, NEW UTRECHT H.S.; VIC HANSON, LONG ISLAND CITY H.S.;
ZEKE SINICOLA, FRANKLIN H.S. AND ABE BECKER, LINCOLN H.S. (COURTESY OF INTERNATIONAL
NEWS PHOTOS) (ABOVE, RIGHT) AT BASKETBALL-MAD TAMARACK LODGE IN THE CATSKILLS, 1948,
BOB (NO. 14) MEETS WITH GEORGE KAFTAN (NO. 12), ANOTHER HOLY CROSS STAR, AND MAX
ZASLOFSKY. (BELOW, LEFT) A GREAT COMPETITOR, BOB HATED TO SWEAT IT OUT ON THE HOLY
CROSS BENCH; BUT ONCE ON THE COURT, HE WOULD UNCOIL LIKE A SPRING, AS SHOWN (BELOW,
RIGHT) IN THE ACTION SHOT OF A GAME BETWEEN HOLY CROSS AND VALPARAISO AT THE BOSTON
GARDEN, 1950. (PHOTOS BY YALE JOEL, COURTESY OF LIFE MAGAZINE)

BOB DEMONSTRATES A TRICK MANEUVER HE'S OCCASIONALLY USED IN A CLUTCH. IN THIS RE
MARKABLE SEQUENCE OF SHOTS HE DRIBBLES TOWARD THE BASKET, PASSES BEHIND HIS BACK TO
THROW A CLOSE-COVERING OPPONENT OFF GUARD, THEN DRIVES IN FOR A SHOT. ALTHOUGH H
WAS ABLE TO PULL THIS TRICK AGAINST LOYOLA WITH ONLY SECONDS REMAINING, HE DOESN'

DVISE USING IT EXCEPT "ON THE SPUR OF A DESPERATE MOMENT." WHEN THE CELTICS GREW IRED OF "SWEETWATER" CLIFTON'S HATFUL OF TRICKS, BOB PUT ON HIS OWN EXHIBITION FOR HE BENEFIT OF THE KNICKS' STALWART BY RUNNING THE BALL UP ONE ARM AND DOWN THE THER. FROM THEN ON "SWEETWATER PLAYED US STRAIGHT." (PHOTO BY GEORGE WOODRUFF)

(ABOVE) BOB, HIS WIFE MISSIE, AND THEIR TWO DAUGHTERS, MARY PATRICIA, 4, AND MARIE COLETTE, 5, ENJOY A FAMILY HUDDLE AT CAMP GRAYLAG, PITTSFIELD, N.H., DURING THE SUMMER OF 1956. THE CELTICS STAR, WHO HAS BEEN RUNNING THE ATHLETIC PROGRAM AT THE BOYS' CAMP, PLANS TO CONTINUE WORKING WITH YOUNGSTERS IN THE YEARS TO COME. (PHOTO BY DICK HANLEY) (BELOW) BOB RECEIVES THE MOST VALUABLE PLAYER AWARD FROM MAURICE PODOLOFF, PRESIDENT OF THE NATIONAL BASKETBALL ASSOCIATION, IMMEDIATELY FOLLOWING THE EAST-WEST ALL-STAR CONTEST IN THE BOSTON GARDEN ON JANUARY 15, 1957. THAT WAS THE GAME IN WHICH HIS TEAMMATE BILL SHARMAN SANK A BASKET FROM 70 FEET OUT. (COURTESY OF RUSS ADAMS, BOSTON HERALD)

I didn't know her very well, and when I thought about her at all, it was only as a real pretty girl who was out of my reach.

None of the guys I went around with was friendly with any of her crowd until just before we graduated from high school. Then, during the summer that I was at Tamarack Lodge prior to entering Holy Cross, a friend of mine named Mike Schmidt began taking Missie out. And after I got back from the Catskills, Mike and Missie went out on a few double dates with Joan Kilduff and me.

The more I saw of Missie, the better I liked her. We went out on only a few of these double dates at the end of the summer of 1946 because I had to go away to college. Joan and I corresponded, but whenever I got home, I always made sure that all our dates were double ones with Missie and Mike. And once we got to wherever we were going, I always managed to sit beside Missie so we could talk.

Finally, one night during Christmas vacation I said, "Look, why don't you go out with me some night?"

"Because you haven't asked me," she said.

"Well, I'm asking you now."

We went together for the next three years. Missie came to Holy Cross dances, went to Holy Cross basketball games and knew all my Holy Cross friends. Early in my junior year, when I was home for a weekend, we began talking about getting married.

"How about the night of the Junior Prom?" I suggested.

"While you're still a junior?" she said. "That wouldn't make any sense. Let's wait until you graduate."

So she talked me out of a Junior Prom wedding. And within a year it looked as if we'd talked each other out of any wedding at all.

Except for my crush on Joan Kilduff, I had played the field up to the time I started going with Missie. Then I dropped all the other girls I knew. Missie and I went steady for over two years.

But during my senior year, we drifted apart. In St. Albans, Missie discovered she had new interests, and I discovered that Worcester had a generous collection of attractive girls.

Frank Oftring, one of my basketball teammates, had become my closest pal at Holy Cross. He was from Brooklyn but seemed to know everyone in Worcester. Up to my senior year, I'd been so wrapped up in Missie that I wasn't interested in anyone else. But now Frank and I discovered we had more interests than we could handle.

Frank, a tall, lanky guy with a perpetual smile on his face, had gone about everywhere I went to play basketball, including Tamarack. Now I started going everywhere he went and not to play basketball. Usually we went out in pairs, but sometimes other guys went along. As my senior year in college progressed, I thought less and less about marriage. I had too much else on my mind.

But Missie and I had practically agreed to get married in June, right after I got my college degree. This was something I had looked forward to with great anticipation up to about Christmas time. But by then I was beginning to wonder if it was such a good idea. And the more I wondered, the more convinced I was that it wasn't.

In the meantime, Frank and Bob McMullen, another guy on the Holy Cross basketball team, had discovered a cabin on Lake Webster, right outside Worcester, which they could rent for a song. They asked me if I wanted to go in with them.

"This," I said, "sounds like a great idea. Only I'm supposed to get married in June—or am I?"

At this point Frank and I were in the process of arranging to open a gas station in Worcester in September. We also had other plans for making a buck. My head was spinning with ideas. And between the cabin on Lake Webster, the gas station and the vague plans for building up the Cousy fortunes, I didn't see any purpose in rushing into marriage right after I got out of college. I didn't know it, but Missie was thinking along the same lines.

She was staying with her sister in Groton, Massachusetts, not far from Worcester. One day in the spring of 1950, I said rather tentatively, "What do you think about postponing our wedding until fall?"

She looked at me sort of funny and said, "I was just going to ask you to do that."

I did a double take.

"Let's be sure, Bob," she said.

Now, I was really upset. My pride was hurt because I figured I had control of the situation. But Missie was the one who had taken over.

I tried to backtrack. "Well, maybe we ought to get married in June at that," I said.

"Maybe we ought not," Missie said firmly. "I don't want to rush into anything."

I started seeing red. I made a nasty crack, and she came back with one of her own. We got madder and madder, and our nice little talk developed into a Grade A fight. And when I walked out of there, it looked as if the ball game was over. Our engagement was broken.

I didn't see Missie again for months. I took another girl to the Senior Ball at Holy Cross and moved into the cabin with Oftring and McMullen a few days after we graduated. The three of us had a terrific time for five or six weeks. But by the end of July I was very restless. I wouldn't admit it to anyone but myself, but I missed Missie something terrible. I was sick of playing the field. It wasn't so easy to find a girl with whom you'd want to spend the rest of your life. And to make matters worse, I heard Missie was going out with another guy in St. Albans.

I could have kicked myself for being such a knucklehead. If I'd had any brains, I might have been married to Missie in June. So I put my pride in my pocket and sat down and wrote her a letter. I told her I wanted to see her and asked her when we could get together.

She didn't answer for about ten days. Then she sent me a birthday card. On it was a short note, telling me she had a job in Winchendon, Massachusetts, less than an hour out of Worcester if you drive fast enough.

I dropped everything and headed for Winchendon. I guess I was lucky to get there alive. I broke every speed record ever set up by the Commonwealth of Massachusetts and made it in something like half an hour. When I got to Winchendon and called Missie, I was ready to get down on my knees and beg her forgiveness.

"I was a dope," I said. "Please, honey, one more chance?"

"One more chance," she said.

They were the nicest words I'd heard all summer.

From then on I was the wet blanket in the cabin on Lake Webster. I wouldn't go out with anyone but Missie, which meant I spent most of my time around Winchendon. Oftring and McMullen had to get along by themselves for the rest of the summer.

| CHAPTER | 12 | *Wedding bells* |

THREE WEEKS AFTER OUR REUNION MISSIE AND I WERE EN-
gaged again. By this time I knew I wanted to live perma-
nently in Worcester. When the summer was over, I took a
room with Al and Helen Kalil, a Syrian couple, who were
close friends of mine. I also acquired a police dog named
Beauty, who accompanied me everywhere, except to the Boston Garden, where the Celtics played their home games. I
wanted to take Beauty, but I didn't dare. I was having enough
troubles trying to make the ball club.

Both Missie and I were anxious to get married, but I was
all tied up with the Celtics. That year the National Basketball
Association was making constant schedule changes. We
wanted to set a date that was an off-day for the club, and if
we couldn't do that, at least a day when the team was playing in Boston during a home stand.

November 18 looked like the best time. The Celtics would
be back from a road trip, and it was a day off before a couple
of games in Boston. Missie agreed to that date, and in our
innocence we actually believed we could get married then.

But one of the teams in the league folded or something, and the schedule was reshuffled. Our wedding got lost in the shuffle because the Celtics had to play out west somewhere on the night of November 18. We postponed the date to December 3, but another schedule change landed the Celtics' out of town again.

"Honey," I said, "we've got to pick a date that isn't so far in advance. Then the league won't have time to change its mind."

We checked the schedule again, a document that Missie was beginning to loathe. We finally decided on December 9. The Celtics were playing in Boston, and it was less than a week away. It was too late for a change so the date was safe. I don't know what would have happened if there had been another change. By this time poor Missie was frantic.

We had long since rented an apartment in Worcester, and I was living there alone with Beauty, my police dog. With a fairly sure wedding date set, I rushed arrangements. Through the Kalils, I hired the Syrian-American Club in Worcester for the wedding reception. I called Father Tiernan, who was officiating, and he arranged for the ceremony to be performed at St. Peter's Church at ten o'clock in the morning. A caterer agreed to provide a formal breakfast, complete with champagne.

Frank Oftring, the best man, went out and got cuff links and ties for the ushers. I designated one of them, Jim Duffley, to call for Missie on the morning of the wedding and escort her to the church. She and her mother were coming in the night before to stay at the apartment with Beauty, who loved Missie as much as she loved me, while I moved in with friends.

On the night before the wedding the ushers helped Frank and me arrange the tables and chairs at the Syrian-American

Club so that we would have as much open space as possible for dancing.

Everything was set. If there were no hitches, this would be a nice, smooth, uneventful wedding, a fitting climax to a four-year romance, complete with lovers' quarrel. I went to bed the night before happy and secure in the knowledge that after all the snags things would now go beautifully.

I didn't know the half of it. The wedding of Marie Ritterbusch and Robert J. Cousy on the morning of December 9, 1950, was a classic of marvelous confusion. In my craziest dreams I never pictured the possibility of so many things going wrong.

I woke up early and, of course, nervous. I got dressed and paced around until 8:45, when I went out for a haircut. The barber was in no hurry, but I managed to convince him I was, and he got me out of there at 9:15. This gave me three-quarters of an hour to get home, get dressed and get to the church.

But when I walked out, I found my car hemmed in so tightly between two other cars that I couldn't get out. My natural nervousness plus my growing concern about getting to the church on time gave me superhuman strength. I pushed the cars out of the way in a couple of minutes, jumped into my own and rushed home, arriving there a few minutes after 9:30.

I expected to find Oftring waiting for me, but I should have known he wouldn't be. Frank has never been on time for anything in his life, and my wedding day was no exception. And since he had the ties and the cuff links for the ushers, they couldn't make the church until he did. I rushed to my room and threw on my clothes, including striped pants and long morning coat, then rushed downstairs.

Frank strolled in at 9:45. Now we had fifteen minutes to

get ourselves and all those guys to St. Peter's, and they didn't even have their ties or cuff links on. By the time everyone had struggled into wedding gear, it was 10:03. We dived into cars and barreled off to the church, six or seven crowded blocks away. We made it in five minutes. It was exactly 10:08 when I walked up the church steps.

We were late, but things seemed to be more or less under control. There was only one thing wrong. Missie hadn't arrived.

I talked to half a dozen people, but nobody had seen her come in. I got hold of Father Tiernan, and he hadn't seen her either. A funeral which preceded our wedding was just winding up when we got there so we would have had to wait a little while anyway, but now that was ending, and there was another funeral scheduled for 11:00.

I went to the sacristy, but Missie wasn't there. Now I was really worried. I came out the front door of the church again and said to nobody in particular, "Where the heck is Missie?"

The ushers were all standing there, and as I marched around like a caged lion, I suddenly noticed Jim Duffley. I bounced over to him and screamed, "Jim, where's Missie?"

"I don't know," he said.

"Well, if you don't, who does?" I howled. "Jim, for the love of Mike, don't you remember—you're supposed to pick her up and escort her to the church!"

"Good Lord!" he groaned, "I forgot all about it!"

He and another usher jumped into a car and rushed for the apartment while I paced around some more. Later I found out what happened when they got there.

Dressed in her wedding gown, poor Missie was in tears. She and her mother were thinking about getting the next train to St. Albans when the boys rang the doorbell. But as she let them in, Missie let Beauty out. The big dog bounded out the front door and into a clump of bushes in front of the apartment. The boys went after her, but she wouldn't pay any attention. Finally Missie went out in her wedding gown and coaxed Beauty in. She had to grab her in the process, and as the party rushed back to the church, Missie's mother was frantically picking burs off her gown.

They got to St. Peter's at 10:30, and the Mass had already started. I breathed a long sigh of relief when I saw Missie get out of the car, but I ducked out of sight. She had obviously been crying, and her mother was obviously mad. Mrs. Ritterbusch and I have since become very close, but that morning she glared at me with curdling looks that made me want to shrivel.

At last the ceremony got under way. When the last words had been repeated and I kissed Missie, my one thought was, "Now, she is my wife, and I know we're going to be happy." I was in a delicious daze as we walked back up the aisle.

It didn't last long. It was 11:05 when we walked out of the church, the central figures in a happy, chattering crowd, made up almost exclusively of young people throwing confetti and rice and old shoes. Photographers were waiting to get pictures of the bride and groom, and there was a big crowd of well-wishers out on the sidewalk.

I didn't see any of it. Neither did Missie. Instead, both of us were staring in morbid fascination at the first thing that greeted us on the landing of the church steps—the casket for the funeral to follow!

The steps of the church were alive with people—and such a mixture of people I've never seen before or since! Laughing, cheering wedding guests on their way out were bumping into mourners on their way in. While youngsters were boisterously shouting congratulations, bewildered elderly men and women were angrily muttering, "Have they no respect for the dead?"

Before we headed for the Syrian-American Club, Missie and I stopped at the home of Al and Jane Vieraitis, who'd prepared an elaborate breakfast for the wedding party. As events turned out, it was a good thing they fortified us in advance.

When we finally got into a car to drive to the Syrian-American Club for the reception, I remember saying to Missie, "Don't worry, honey. There won't be anything wrong from now on. I've got everything fixed."

"I'll bet," she said before kissing me.

Everything at the Syrian-American Club was fixed just dandy. When Missie and I walked into the place, the band erupted in a waltz for the two of us to dance to. It was very cozy. The caterers had rearranged the tables so that instead of a lot of dancing space there was practically no space at all. Missie in her wedding gown and I in my swallow-tail must have looked lovely waltzing around tables and chairs and tripping over furniture when we missed.

When the waltz was over and I turned to the tables, I was horrified. Instead of individual servings, there were heaping platters of cold food, and all the plates were bare. In order to eat, everyone had to dig into the platters. Our nice formal wedding breakfast looked like a boarding-house bender.

I turned to one of the waiters and said, "Where's the lady in charge?"

The guy shrugged. "I don't know," he said. "I only work here."

"Well, where's whoever's in charge?" I demanded.

The waiter pointed to a little guy in one corner of the room. I called him over and said, "This is terrible. What happened to the breakfast I ordered? And where's the lady I ordered it from?"

"She's in the hospital," the little guy said laconically.

"What happened?"

"The oven blew up," he said.

Frank Oftring leaned over in front of Missie and whispered, "We're going to have to toast you in tomato juice."

"Why?"

"No champagne," he said.

"But I ordered it."

"It must have blown up with the oven," said Frank.

So we got toasted in tomato juice.

We didn't have champagne, but there was plenty of other liquid refreshment available. By the time we had to leave to go into town, the wedding guests were feeling no pain. Walter Brown, the Celtics' owner, had sent twenty-five tickets for the game that night so half the wedding party went to Boston and continued the party at the Garden.

Missie and I left the reception at about four in the afternoon. I had to get to the Boston Garden for the basketball game. Missie sat with the other Celtics wives and watched us get murdered by Syracuse. Then we drove from the Garden to the Hotel Kenmore. That was our wedding trip. Two nights later the Celtics left for an eight-day road trip.

I have often wondered since why Missie married me.

I3 *Houdini of the Hardwoods*

THE RESPONSIBILITIES OF MARRIAGE AND POTENTIAL FAtherhood weighed so heavily on me that I didn't waste too much time trying to figure out new ways to make money. My professional basketball career was just beginning with the Celtics, and I wasn't doing badly, but I wanted to find something that would supplement my income.

I finally ended up with a partnership in Camp Graylag in Pittsfield, N.H., a boys' camp which has worked out very well in the past few years. But before I got into the camp business I tried my oversized hands at a number of things, practically all of which rolled over and died on me.

Frank Oftring and I had planned the gas station for a long time, but we didn't actually open it until September, 1951. The opening was a doozer. We had more partners than gas because neither of us had the dough to swing the thing alone. The station was at the corner of Main and Piedmont Streets, about half a mile from the center of town, and we called it "Cousy and Oftring."

We started like a house afire. Opening day was a flag-bedecked fiesta with hundreds of cars actually standing in line while Frank and I helped run the pumps. Neither of us knew much about it, but every customer asked for us, and we had to be on hand. There was a band which somebody dug up somewhere, and all the Holy Cross athletes who were still around Worcester showed up. The Worcester *Gazette* gave us great coverage with pictures and stories, and there was even a radio broadcast right from the scene.

It looked like we were home free. All we had to do, we figured, was keep our names up there where people could see them and show up every day. And if we couldn't show up, we had plenty of partners to show up for us.

We did great business for two days. Then the novelty wore off. Cousy and Oftring, the Holy Cross basketball stars, quickly became a couple of local guys running a gas station and not a very good one at that. We couldn't cut prices, we didn't know enough about fixing cars to become mechanics, and we weren't around enough to check on the profits. It soon became evident that "Cousy and Oftring" was not going to be a gold mine for the partners so we set up an auto driving school.

We operated from the gas station, and for a time the project worked out all right. A year and a half later we sold our interest in the gas station, which is now being run under more competent management, and about the same time I sold Frank my interest in the driving school. He ran it for a few years and then gave it up.

Long before I took over a share in Camp Graylag, I was thinking about getting into camp work. A Holy Cross friend of mine named Jimmy O'Connell had the same idea, and the two of us began looking for camp sites in the winter of 1952. We didn't find any, but through Jimmy I met Joe Sharry, who has since become my partner in the insurance business and one of my closest friends.

Joe, a slightly-built guy a little older than I, was in the insurance business. He was a basketball fan who had known me by reputation before we met. The first time I saw him, we talked about ideas in general but nothing in particular. He pointed out that I should take advantage of my basketball name while I could, and we made a date to get together again. We eventually became involved in a promotion venture which provided me with so many laughs that I almost forgot it cost both Joe and me a pretty substantial bit of change.

We both decided that the most obvious way to take advantage of my basketball reputation was to play basketball. I was so daffy about the game I could play it any time, anywhere and under any conditions. My mistake was that I thought other people were just as daffy. This little miscalculation cost me a few dollars before I was through, but maybe I got a few dollars' worth of laughs. So I guess I ended up even.

After the basketball season ended in the spring of 1952, Sharry and I took our wives on a vacation to Hyannis on Cape Cod. While there, we checked around and found that the number of summer visitors to the Cape area ran into the hundreds of thousands and most of them, so we were told, had nothing to do in the evenings.

"Let's give them something to do," said Joe.

"I know just the thing!" I said enthusiastically. "Let's give them basketball! We'll get up a couple of good teams and have exhibition games every week. We'll make thousands!"

"Millions," Joe nodded.

So we checked around some more, and everyone with whom we checked seemed to think it was a good idea. A priest by the name of Father Ed Duffy went even further.

"The Cape," he solemnly said, "will be electrified."

The Cape was electrified all right. It was electrified to the point where I lost seven thousand dollars in two summers. I was lucky to get out alive.

Basketball in the summer! Even today, I can't see how it would miss. But after what happened to us on the Cape I wouldn't touch it again with a ten-foot pole.

Sharry and I found a spot on the main road outside Hyannis that looked perfect for outdoor basketball games. We took a lease on land which had promise—if you were an optimist. It was across the street from a police station and next door to a place where they had weekly wrestling matches.

The land we leased was just land; we had to convert it into a basketball court. We got Frank Oftring to help us blacktop so we'd have a nice hard surface. We rented stands from Durfee High School in New Bedford. For a fence we used a big section of canvas, and we hired lights, figuring we'd start games at 8:00 P.M.

This was going to be the scene of Wednesday night games between Bob Cousy's All-Stars and any opponents we could find. The backbone of Bob Cousy's All-Stars looked familiar to anyone who had ever watched Holy Cross in action. Oftring, Laska and Curran played for me along with a good friend of mine from Fall River named Andy Farrissey. Joe and I were always on the lookout for anyone else we could find. We never knew when we'd end up with only four players, a most embarrassing situation when you've got a basketball game to play.

One day as we were driving down to the Cape from Worcester in Joe's convertible, we were worrying about that very problem. At the junction of Route 9, the Worcester-Boston turnpike, and Route 128 a cutoff road around Boston which we always took to get to the Cape, we saw a great big guy hitchhiking toward Boston. We pulled up beside him, and I asked, "Hey, buddy, how tall are you?"

"Six feet, four," he said.

"You play basketball?"

"Sure. I'm on the —— team."

He named a junior college which I'd never heard of, but I was satisfied. A guy that tall had to be a basketball player.

"How would you like to make a fast ten bucks?" I asked.

"I'm so broke," he said, "I'd settle for a slow ten bucks."

"O.K., jump in. We need a basketball player for an exhibition game on Cape Cod tonight."

So the guy forgot he was headed for Boston and got in beside us. Naturally we talked basketball.

"Come from around here?" asked Joe.

The guy nodded.

"Ever watch the Celtics play?"

"Sure."

"Who's your favorite Celtics ballplayer?" I asked.

"Macauley," he said. "That guy's the greatest."

"How about that showoff Cousy?" I asked.

"A bum."

"Notice what a pig he is?" said Joe. "Always shooting for baskets and publicity. Never throws a pass to anyone else."

"A pig," the guy said. "A real pig."

"Doesn't belong in the same league with Macauley," I remarked.

"No, sir. That Macauley's a real pro."

"But not Cousy," I said.

"Not Cousy."

"Just a good college player," Sharry commented.

The guy shook his head vigorously. Then he said, "Not even that."

We drove along in silence for a few minutes. Then Joe said, "Take a good look at that guy on your left."

The big guy turned toward me but didn't show any signs of recognition.

"Ever seen him before?" Joe asked.

"Nope, can't say as I have," he said.

"Well," said Joe. "His name is Cousy. Bob Cousy."

For a minute, I thought the big guy was going to cry. He started to apologize, but Joe and I laughed it off, and I asked him how good a basketball player he was. It was a leading question. He spent the next hour and a half telling us. By the time we arrived in Hyannis we thought we had another George Mikan, which he wasn't.

We got our court in Hyannis set up for a July 3 opening. We were going to play two nights in a row against a team from Connecticut. Joe and I went down to the Cape the weekend before to try to steam up some interest in the game. We distributed circulars outside a movie one night, then on Sunday each of us went to the two nearest Catholic churches and distributed more as people came out. We caught every Mass from seven in the morning until twelve. We also hired kids to throw circulars into parked cars.

On the day of the game we got down to the Cape early in Joe's car. He had it plastered with posters and pictures of me, labeled "Houdini of the Hardwoods" and "Magic Marvel." We started in Falmouth and rode along the beach areas all the way to Hyannis with the convertible decked out like a circus wagon and Joe hawking the game through a loudspeaker he had hired in Worcester.

"Come to the basketball game in Hyannis tonight and see the Houdini of the Hardwoods!" he bawled. "See the great Bob Cousy in action personally and in the flesh! The Magic

Marvel will be in the basketball game in Hyannis tonight!"

It was too much for me. Long before we reached Hyannis I ducked into the back seat and tried to block up my ears.

Right in the middle of this exhibition (which was probably worth more money than the basketball game) Joe said in a stage whisper, "I'm going to drop by the newspaper office in the next block. You hold the fort."

I raised my head and peeked out as Joe pulled into a parking space. People were walking by, and a few stopped to look at our rig. Just before Joe got out he said, "Hey, Bob, one of the posters is loose. While I'm in there, plaster it back."

By this time a little crowd had gathered, but I was never one to shirk a duty. I climbed out of the car and started taping up the picture of myself. Suddenly, to my horror, a little girl pointed at me and screamed, "Hey, Mister, are you the Houdini of the Hardwoods?"

I turned and fled after Joe.

We got to the court at six o'clock that night. We had to sweep both court and stands, set up ticket booths, put the cloth around the place and get everything ready by eight o'clock. We picked up a couple of kids to help us, and I went over to the police station across the street to make sure everything was all right there. The cops had the only shower in the neighborhood and had given us permission to use it. We were also permitted to dress there.

We charged $1.80 a ticket and figured we would draw maybe as many as three thousand people. How could anyone resist the Houdini of the Hardwoods on the night before the Fourth in Hyannis? Hyannis and its surroundings, it turned out, were full of resisters. By game time there weren't more than one hundred people in the stands. We waited until about 8:30, then with about three hundred paid, we played the game.

It was a terribly windy night. You couldn't shoot from more than fifteen feet out from the basket. Neither team was very enthusiastic, but we had to keep running to stay warm so it wasn't the worst game in the world. Before it was over Sharry had let kids into the place for whatever change they had in their pockets, but that hardly swelled the crowd.

It was far from an inspirational beginning, but it was better than nothing. We raised enough to pay the $150 guarantee we'd promised the other team. After the game everyone but Sharry and me went across the street to the police station to shower and dress. We had to pay off players, officials and the opposing team, take the cloth down, clean up and count the money.

And that, we discovered, wasn't all. The station house shower leaked, and there was half a foot of water on the floor. Joe and I had to mop up the joint so the cops would let us use it again the next night.

That was the night of the second game of the series with the team from Connecticut. Those guys weren't dopes. They knew we were in trouble. So instead of showing up on the court at game time, they sat in their cars, waiting to see how many people paid their way in. It was another windy night, and by eight o'clock, there wasn't a soul in the stands. Half an hour later, about ten customers were clapping their hands in unison and yelling for action. The Houdini of the Hardwoods was dressing in the police station and wishing he were dead. His partner was at the basketball court with one eye on the stands and the other on his watch. When I came out, Joe pulled me into a dark corner and whispered, "Those other guys are still in their cars. If we don't get some people in here by nine, I'm going to call the game off."

Not another soul showed up. At nine sharp, Sharry snapped off the lights and announced, "The other team has not appeared. The game is off. Money will be refunded at the box office."

I have seen rhubarbs in my time but never one like this. While the ten customers rushed to the change booth to get their dough back, the guys on the Connecticut team poured out of their cars and bleated for their $50 guarantee. Missie and Frank Oftring's wife, both very pregnant, were with us, and if they hadn't been, I guess those characters would have killed us. We stood in the middle of the blacked-out court arguing over the guarantee for an hour, and we'd be there yet, I suppose, except that July 4 fireworks started in the place next door and the sparks landed on us. We all had to get out of there before we burned to death.

It was a pretty horrible beginning, and if I'd had any brains, it would have been the end. But we kept going all summer and were even daffy enough to try it again the summer after. That time we had a backer, but my conscience is clear. Joe and I told him it was a bad investment, and he insisted on going in anyhow. He saw all our books and knew we'd lost our shirts the year before.

I still thought it could be put over if we only ballyhooed it properly. We gave it the best we had. Once Joe even hired an airplane and rode with the pilot while he tried to skywrite "See the Houdini of the Hardwoods at Hyannis tonight." But it was a windy day, and the message was blown out to sea. It cost us fifty bucks, but I got that much in laughs. I stood on the beach and collapsed at the sight of poor Joe holding his tummy in that bouncing plane while one of his brightest ideas literally went up in smoke.

I4 *Suspense*

I MAY HAVE BEEN THE HOUDINI OF THE HARDWOODS AND charter member of the Fancy Pants A.C. in college, but the pro teams didn't try any harder to get me than the colleges had after I got out of high school. It was the same old story. They all thought I was too small. At six feet, one and a half, I just wasn't built like a professional basketball player.

Naturally I wanted to play for the Boston Celtics. Worcester had become my home, and the Celtics were my team. It was an easy commute to Boston—although there were times when the Celtics' front office wasn't so sure—and I had played many games in the Boston Garden, which was the "home" court for Holy Cross when I was there. I knew Walter Brown well and was a great admirer of his.

During my last year at college Doggie Julian was the Celtics coach. However, I figured we'd get along all right. I had grown up a little since I'd had my differences with him, and I was sure he held nothing against me. But before I got out of school Doggie made another shift. He became the Dart-

127

mouth College basketball coach, and the Celtics were taken over by Arnold (Red) Auerbach.

When I read about the shift, I didn't have time to think much about it. I was too busy with college exams and plans for the summer in the cabin on Lake Webster. It looked like a break for me—that's all I knew. I didn't think I'd get mixed up in any more rhubarbs with Doggie Julian, but I was just as happy to see him out of there.

I had never met Red Auerbach, but he had a terrific coaching reputation for a guy only in his early thirties. Red's college career at George Washington University had not been sensational; he was just another fairly good basketball player. But he was a keen student of the game, and by the time the Celtics hired him, he was considered the best brain in the business. For my money he still is. When he went to Boston, he'd already won a couple of titles with the old Washington Capitols.

This sounded like my kind of guy, and I was delighted with the prospect of playing under him. It never occurred to me that I wouldn't. Obviously, I figured, the Celtics would draft me. They had territorial rights to my services, which meant that they could take me the first time around. If they didn't, it would be open season on Cousy; anybody who drafted me could have me. But this couldn't happen to me. Surely, the Celtics would grab me at the first opportunity.

But when the basketball moguls met in their draft meeting in the spring of 1950—a few days after Auerbach's appointment was announced—imagine my embarrassment, not to say shock, when I learned that the Celtics had passed me up! A reporter phoned and asked for my reaction to the news.

"What news?" I innocently inquired.

"Haven't you heard?" the writer said. "The Celtics didn't take you."

I opened my mouth, but it took a few seconds for any words to come out. "Who did?" I finally managed to ask.

"Tri-Cities," he said.

"Who?"

"Tri-Cities," he repeated.

"Where the devil is Tri-Cities?" I asked hopelessly, then hung up.

Before the day was over I said a lot of other things I shouldn't have said. Among other things, I pointed out that I was planning to operate a gas station and didn't need basketball to make a living. I told one writer that if I didn't play for the Celtics, I wouldn't play for anyone. I told another that I had no intention of trying to find Tri-Cities, much less play for it—or them. And I told other writers a few other things, all adding up to the announcement that the N.B.A. and all its owners and coaches could go, as far as I was concerned.

How could the Celtics do this to me? Why, I had made practically every All-America team and should have been one of the most sought-after basketball players in the country! Would the great Cousy play for something called Tri-Cities? Never!

Twenty-four hours later I began to think straight. The Celtics had selected Chuck Share instead of me the first time around, and it made sense. Share was an All-America center from Bowling Green, a huge man only an inch short of seven feet. Guys like him definitely didn't grow on trees, and the Celtics would have been crazy not to take him under the circumstances.

If I went into the pro league, it would have to be as a backcourt man. I was too short to play up forward. The Celtics had a dozen guys who could play in the back court.

But I went to Boston to see Walter Brown as soon as he got back from the draft meetings.

"Isn't there some way I can play for you?" I asked him. "Boston is my town. The fans here know me. I live only thirty-five miles away. I've been looking forward to playing for the Celtics, and this is a terrible belt. Please do something, Walter."

"I'm sorry, Bob," he said. "I didn't want to make this move, but we had to. We need height, and Share gives it to us. I wish we could have gotten both of you, but it wasn't possible. Besides, we couldn't take a chance on you."

Then he pointed out that the Celtics had been disappointed time after time in New England college basketball players who hadn't made the grade with them. He cited several guys, including three former teammates of mine at Holy Cross: George Kaftan, Dermie O'Connell and Joe Mullaney, all of whom had failed to make it.

"I'd like to have you," he said. "Believe me, I would. You're a big name around here, and the writers and fans are already asking questions. But there isn't anything we can do about it now."

"What do you think I should do?" I asked.

"I can't think of a thing," he said. "You're the property of another team now, and it's against regulations for me to suggest anything. I shouldn't even be talking to you."

So I went back to Worcester, and by the time I reached there, I was curious enough about Tri-Cities to find out that it was a combination of Moline and Rock Island in Illinois and Davenport, Iowa. And a day or so later I was reconciled to the situation.

I didn't even blow my stack when I read what Auerbach was supposed to have said at a press conference a few days later. Someone asked him why he hadn't drafted Cousy. According to the story, he turned to Walter and asked, "Am I supposed to win or worry about the local yokels?"

And Walter was reported to have replied, "Just win."

You can imagine what the Boston sports writers did with that one. There were eight papers in the city at the time, and they'd all been great to me throughout my college career. As far as they were concerned, Cousy could do no wrong. This led to a rather unhappy situation for Red. He has been the target of some local writers ever since. To this day they don't let him forget that he passed me up in the draft. It's unfair because the man is a great coach, but he sacrifices tact for honesty. He'll always be a better coach than a public relations man. He still doen't care what he says or how he says it.

Walter had told me how to get in touch with Ben Kerner, then owner of the Tri-Cities Black Hawks. He had a business in Buffalo, New York, and Brown gave me his phone number. I called Kerner after the shock wore off, and he invited me to go to Buffalo to talk contract. I flew there from Worcester after classes one day.

Kerner gave me the red carpet treatment. He met me at the airport in his new convertible and drove me around town. Then he let me have the car for the afternoon and arranged to meet me at a night club for dinner. Up to then neither of us had mentioned a word about my contract.

Finally, after a very good meal indeed, Ben sat back in his chair, looked at me and said, "Well, I guess you want to talk a little business now."

"I guess I do."

"What did you have in mind in the way of salary?" he asked.

"What did *you* have in mind?" I countered.

We fenced for a while. Then Ben said, "Bob, you're a young fellow, and you won't even be out of college for a month or so. I'm ready to pay you what I think you're worth at this time."

I didn't say anything.

"I'll give you $6,500," he said.

I stood up.

"Drive me back to the airport," I said.

"Now take it easy," Ben said. "Just sit down and calm yourself. $6,500 is a lot of money for a twenty-one-year-old kid. It's more than most men in the league get."

"It's not enough for me," I said.

"What is?" he asked.

"$10,000," I said.

He stood up.

"O.K.," he said. "I'll drive you back to the airport."

Back in Worcester I stewed, but I stuck to my guns. I had decided to ask for $10,000, and that was the figure to which I intended to stick. Kerner phoned me a day or so later and said he was prepared to go up if I'd come down.

"Look," I said, "I'm not a very good businessman. If I were, I'd have asked for $12,000 and come down to ten. But ten is what I want, and I won't play for any less than that."

There were more phone calls as the days went by until finally Kerner went up to about $7,500. I still insisted that I wanted ten thousand and that didn't mean a dime less. Then one day he phoned and said, "All right, Bob, come on up to Buffalo. Everything's O.K."

I took the first plane I could get, and there was Ben waiting for me at the airport. He shook hands cordially as I stepped off the plane, then as we walked toward his shiny new convertible, he said, "Well, Bob, what's your situation?"

I stopped dead in my tracks.

"What do you mean, what's my situation?" I said. "You know my situation. I thought you said everything was O.K."

"Everything is," he said. "Now come on down to my office and we'll get it all straightened out."

But I was mad. I wanted to go right back to Worcester, and he had quite a time getting me into his car. When we got to his office, there was another guy there whom Ben introduced.

"We can talk freely with him," Ben said. "He's a partner of mine."

So we talked freely for about three hours. It was the same old story. Back and forth we went, going over the same arguments dozens of times and always coming to the same conclusions. Kerner wanted me to play for $7,500; I wouldn't budge from my demand for ten thousand.

Then he said, "Bob, you're crazy. Don't you realize as a single man how much tax you'd have to pay? I can show you where you're better off tax-wise at $7,500 than at $10,000."

That one broke me up. I started laughing, and so did Kerner's partner. Even Ben couldn't keep a straight face.

We talked some more, then Kerner said, "All right. Let's ask him. He's an impartial observer."

"Your partner?" I said. "An impartial observer?"

Ben grinned, then said, "Well, let's ask him anyhow."

So we asked the partner. And to my surprise the guy said, "Bob's right. He ought to get more money. Give him $9,000."

"Well—" said Kerner. "It's a lot of money—more than I intended to pay. But I'll tell you, Bob. He says $9,000 so it's O.K. with me. How about you?"

My resistance was gone. By that time all I wanted to do was get it over with. I agreed to $9,000. Kerner called the papers, a couple of photographers took pictures of me signing and then we all went out to dinner. I went back to Worcester that night and for the time being forgot about Kerner, Tri-Cities and the National Basketball Association. I had a gas station to open, wild oats to sow and a lost girl friend to get back.

The summer passed and so did much of September before I heard from Kerner again. By this time I was engaged to Missie, but we couldn't set a wedding date until I knew where and when I was supposed to report for practice. As far as I knew, I was still with Tri-Cities and vaguely wondering whether Moline, Rock Island or Davenport would provide the best love nest for a couple of newly-weds.

I didn't know it, but I was getting tossed around the league like a yo-yo. I found out later that I was with three different teams before I put on a uniform.

It all began when Kerner traded me to the Chicago Stags for Gene Vance. But before the season opened the Stags folded. Maurice Podoloff, president of the N.B.A., called a special meeting in New York to distribute the Chicago players. I don't know how it was done, but I do know that everyone was finally accounted for except Max Zaslofsky, Andy Phillip, and me, with each one of us to go to the Celtics, the New York Knickerbockers or the Philadelphia Warriors.

Everyone wanted Zaslofsky. He was a proven star who had made the league all-star team the previous four years in a row. The Knickerbockers were particularly anxious to get him because he was Jewish and could pull in plenty of fans of that faith while playing in New York.

Phillip was almost as much in demand. He was also a veteran who had long since made his mark in the league. He had been on a couple of all-star teams, and was one of the best play-makers in the business.

Cousy? That razzle-dazzle kid from Holy Cross? Who could tell whether he was any good or not? He was the last on the list as usual, the guy nobody wanted.

The argument over Zaslofsky lasted far into the night. By midnight, Podoloff was still presiding over a stalemate. No one could agree as to who was going to get Zaslofsky. Finally

Podoloff had an inspiration. The three names would be put into a hat, and the owners of the teams involved would pull them out.

Walter Brown drew first, and my name was on the slip. So the Celtics literally pulled my name out of a hat. Incidentally, the Knickerbockers got Zaslofsky that way, and the Warriors ended up with Phillip.

Of course, I was blissfully unaware of all this. All I knew was that practice was slated to begin, and I hadn't heard from anyone. I was packed and ready to take off for Tri-Cities or wherever it was that they trained. I knew that sooner or later I'd hear from Kerner. After all, he was paying me $9,000.

I had moved in with my Syrian friends, Al and Helen Kalil and was sitting around waiting for Kerner to call. But when he did phone, he didn't tell me much.

"Don't go anywhere," he said. "I'll call you again and let you know when to come out."

So I didn't go anywhere. The weeks went by and so did the month of September, and still no more word from Kerner. I was just beginning to wonder how he expected to get his money's worth out of me when he called me the first week in October.

"Your car all packed?" he asked.

I told him it was.

"Good," he said. "Drive it to New York."

"New York?"

"Yes. We're having a league meeting here."

"Am I supposed to go to the meeting?" I asked.

"No. But come down here. And let me know where I can reach you in a hurry," Kerner said.

"I'll be at my mother's house in St. Albans," I told him.

"I'll call you there at six o'clock tonight," he said.

I tried to pump him, but he wouldn't tell me anything more.

But as I drove to New York from Worcester, I was pretty sure of one thing: evidently I wasn't going to have to live in Moline, Rock Island or Davenport. Otherwise Kerner would have told me to go out there.

I got to my mother's about three in the afternoon and kicked around St. Albans for the next couple of hours. We sat down to dinner when my father got home from work. It was about six then, and I was waiting for that call from Kerner.

But it didn't come at six or seven—or eight—or nine. We all sat around the house, and every time the phone rang, I jumped. The hours clicked off, and still Kerner didn't call. I was just thinking of going to bed when the phone started going. The bell exploded like a bomb. It was after midnight.

I grabbed the receiver, and a familiar voice asked, "Bob?"

"Yeah," I said.

"Walter Brown. Get in your car and drive back to Boston. You're with us."

15 *Red*

I LET OUT A "YIPPIE!" AND ASKED NO QUESTIONS. WE JUST talked a few more seconds. I was so excited I wanted to take off then and there. But I spent the night in St. Albans and headed for Boston the next morning.

On the way up I tried to figure out how it had all happened. Remember, up to that time I thought I was still with Tri-Cities and was waiting to hear from Kerner. I didn't find out about the trade to Chicago or the pulling of my name from a hat until I read the Boston papers the next day. All I could think of was "Now I'm home! This is it!"

I still didn't know Red Auerbach, and didn't meet him until late that afternoon. In the meantime, he was quoted in an afternoon paper which I read as soon as I got into town.

"Cousy," he said, "is going to have to make the ball club."

I couldn't help but wonder a little. This guy, I figured, must be tough. Obviously I was going to have to make the ball club, but coming out publicly this way made it look as if I'd have to try harder than the next guy. I wondered if being Bob Cousy might do me more harm than good. It looked as if Auerbach resented anyone from a local college and me in particular. But I met him with an open mind. And five minutes after we'd chatted, I knew we were going to hit it off.

Red is an average-sized guy with a rapidly receding line of red hair. It was receding even then. He has deep brown eyes that bore through you the way Buster Sheary's did, but he didn't remind me of Buster. Sheary was stocky and solid-looking; Auerbach is slight. Sheary was a dedicated, trusting soul who could infuse inspiration into you by sheer force of will. Auerbach is just as dedicated, but he has a hard practicality. Sheary draws you to him; Auerbach tries to repel. Sheary assumes you like him; Auerbach figures you don't.

The result is an interesting contrast of personalities. I felt a deep bond of affection for Buster. I admired Red's ability, but I didn't feel really close to him until I had known him for years. I might add that today we *are* close friends. Contrary to stories that popped up in the newspapers from time to time, we were never enemies nor did we even reach the point of disliking each other.

The worst that happened between Red and me was that I wasn't doing what he wanted me to do my first year with the Celtics, and he in his blunt and tactless way made no bones about saying so. But I didn't resent him then, although outsiders tried to make it appear that I had.

Reports that I had difficulties with Doggie Julian at Holy Cross were true. Reports that I had difficulties with Red Auerbach were absolutely false. Doggie and I went for months without speaking. The moment a story popped about Red and me, Red immediately got hold of me and we talked everything out. There was never a grain of trouble between us.

Naturally I was a little fearful of the reception I'd get from Red. After all, he hadn't tried to cover the fact that he didn't want me in the first place. If Walter Brown had had his way, the Celtics would have drafted me instead of Share. Walter is a softhearted guy and would always let his heart dictate. He knew I wanted to play for the Celtics. Red was the man who told him Share was essential in their scheme of things and that I was not, so he took Share.

Of course, it was Red who fought for Zaslofsky or Phillip over me at the New York meeting when the Chicago players were reassigned to other clubs. And Red was always fighting to get the big, tough man, for he felt that a small team, no matter how clever, couldn't live long in the N.B.A. He was right. The Celtics didn't win a title until 1957, and one reason we finally crashed through was because tall, fast, tough men like Bill Russell, Tommy Heinsohn and Jim Loscutoff blossomed into stars for us.

Since Red had made it so evident that he wasn't crazy about having me on his club, I was more than anxious to prove he was wrong. I put out more for Red than I ever had for any coach. Not that I hadn't put out for Sheary or Julian or Grummond, but I *had* to show Red I could play major league basketball.

The first time I met him he was direct and to the point.

"You're not a big man," he said, "so I can't use you up front. You're going to be in the back court and work with Sonny Herzberg. He knows this league, and he can teach you a lot. Listen to what he says, and do as he tells you."

Then after we had talked half an hour or so, he said, "I hope you make this team. If you can, I'll be glad to have you. If you can't, don't blame me. A little guy always has two strikes on him in this business. It's a big man's game."

It was blunt talk, but it made sense. And the more I got to know Red Auerbach, the more I realized that everything he did with basketball made sense.

Obviously a professional coach has an altogether different job from a college coach. The college coach has to teach his men how to play basketball, correcting mistakes developed in high school and giving boys the fundamentals they might have missed as youngsters. But a pro coach has to assume that All-America or near-All-America players know all this.

The best pro coach is the man who knows what type of men he wants, how to get them and how to make them into a winning team. He must know the other teams in his league like the back of his hand and devise defenses against the best that opposing teams have to offer. The way he handles his men is important but secondary.

Professional basketball players are adults, and the less supervision they get off the court the better. I've never known one stupid enough to try to drink himself out of the league. A pro athlete knows what he can or can't do and how much his system can take. He also knows that his primary job is to show up in time for practice sessions and games and that he's got to be in shape to give everything he's got.

No one realizes these things better than Auerbach. He isn't a policeman, and he doesn't try to check up on his men off the court. But if anyone shows up in anything but top shape, Red lets him know it.

Auerbach's team of 1957, which won the N.B.A. championship, came as close as any to his ideal concept of a perfect unit. He had spent seven years building that team, and in every respect it was *his* team. His critics have said, "Well, how can it be his team when he didn't want Cousy?" The answer is that at the time he got Cousy he had no way of knowing whether Cousy would fit into his plans or not.

In 1950 Cousy was not the basketball player he became later. He was one of the half-dozen shortest men in the league. He was more rugged than he looked, but that was something

Auerbach had to be shown. He was flashy and a good shooter but knew little about playing defense. This didn't mean he couldn't learn, but that again was something Auerbach had to be shown.

Years later Red said, "We got stuck with the greatest player in the league when we drew his name out of a hat." But at the time I wasn't the greatest player in the league or anywhere near it. I was simply a promising kid who might develop into a professional star, provided I could smooth out the rough edges.

Auerbach never failed to point out the rough edges. He made a sort of game out of damning me with faint praise when he talked to Boston newspapermen. If I had a good night and a writer pointed it out to Red, he would say, "Yeah, he scored plenty of points, but he gave away more with his lousy defensive tactics."

If someone said I was shooting well, he'd reply, "Sure, and he's passing like a clown." And if someone remarked about my passing, he'd say, "His passing was all right, but his shooting was off."

Of course, the sports writers gobbled up all this stuff and faithfully reported everything. I'd read it in Worcester when I got up the next morning and burned. *"I'll show this guy,"* I used to mutter, then the next night I'd try to show him.

"You sure know how to get that Cousy mad," someone commented to him one day.

And he answered, "I sure do, don't I?"

Naturally, there was a method in his madness. Red knew my temperament better than I did. He knew I was the kind of guy who couldn't stand failure and who made it his business to do anything he could to prevent it. Red knew that while I rarely showed my feelings on the surface, I burned inside. And he also knew that I was at my best when I was mad.

Throughout this period he never bawled me out. Instead he carefully pulled me aside and showed me what I was doing wrong and how I could make it right. Often I didn't see him between the time I read a direct quote of his in the paper and the next ball game. That gave me all day to stew.

But I never stayed mad. As a matter of fact, it struck me funny after a while because Red, one of the best needlers I have ever known, was happily feeding the writers exactly the kind of material they didn't want to hear. Whenever someone said something good about me, he'd counter with something bad. Most of the time, he didn't mean it. He simply enjoyed getting on the Boston writers' nerves. Some of them haven't forgiven him yet.

It took Red years to say publicly the words I wanted to hear from him: "Cousy is the greatest." After a year or so, he was saying, "Cousy is the greatest play-maker in the league." That was the first season I led the league in assists. Then he conceded, "Cousy is the greatest *little* man in the league." When a Boston writer took issue, he simply pointed to George Mikan of Minneapolis, who was unquestionably the best in the business. When Mikan retired at the end of the 1955 season, somebody went after Red again.

"*Now* is Cousy the greatest?"

And Red slyly replied, "One of the greatest."

It wasn't until last year that he took off all the wraps. It made me feel good, but it didn't help him with the writers. By then it was too late.

When we won the N.B.A. title in 1957, some of the Boston writers insisted that anyone could have won it with that team. A couple even went farther and claimed that we won it the hard way, that we had no business being carried to the seven-game limit in the playoffs, that we should have beaten St.

Louis in four or five games and that Red wasn't handling us properly.

For my money, Red handled us perfectly. And this championship team was all Red's, a fact which his critics forgot to remember. He had hand-picked almost every man on the team he'd been after for seven years.

Of course, Walter Brown, president of the Celtics, handled all the trading. But Brown rarely does anything without consulting Red first, and he lets Auerbach make most of the decisions as to who should be drafted, bought, sold or traded.

Red is one of the sports world's greatest David Harums. He can get more out of a trade and give away less than any man I've ever seen. When he suggests a deal, other club-owners and coaches automatically go easy. If Auerbach wants it, they figure, it must be good for Auerbach, but what does it do to them?

One secret of Red's success around the conference table is his willingness to take a chance. He'll give up a good deal to get the draft rights on a player he wants, even though he isn't sure the man is obtainable. He took that gamble with Share and during that first year it looked as if he'd lost when Share decided not to play in the N.B.A. in 1950. Later, after Share had played a season as a professional, Red decided the Celtics could do without him.

Share went to Fort Wayne in the deal which brought the Celtics one of its greatest stars, Bill Sharman. It was a great deal for us because we got a couple of other ballplayers too. Sharman is the Deadeye Dick of basketball. Share never developed into a star.

But Auerbach took a chance when he told Walter to make that deal in 1951. Sharman had played half a season with the Washington Capitols. When they folded, he was assigned to

Fort Wayne. But his own plans were up in the air because he was playing baseball in the Brooklyn Dodgers' organization. He was wavering between baseball and basketball, and at the time he hadn't made up his mind which to take. Auerbach wanted him anyway. He knew that Sharman had the makings of one of the great basketball players of all time. And as it turned out, the deal looked great since Sharman eventually gave up baseball and has been a key man with us ever since he came to Boston.

Both Auerbach and Brown agreed to take almost exactly the same type of chance on Bill Russell. He's only been in the league half a season, but he already looks like one of the greatest centers in the history of the game. At the time the Celtics obtained the right to dicker with him, there was no guarantee that they could get him. Still, Auerbach urged Brown to compromise where necessary in order to get Russell.

The price was so high that Red would have looked silly if Russell hadn't signed. The Celtics got him from St. Louis for Ed Macauley and Cliff Hagan. They were giving two good ballplayers to a team that knew it could use them in return for a college kid who hadn't made the big league grade and might never be willing to try. Russell, fresh out of the University of San Francisco, where he had been the outstanding player of the 1955-56 season, was on the American Olympic basketball team, and no one knew what he intended to do after he returned from Australia. The Harlem Globetrotters had made him a fat offer, and he hadn't turned it down yet.

Auerbach was willing to take a chance, and it paid off handsomely. Big, strong, fast and clever, Russell turned out to be almost everything a pro basketball center must be. When he learns to shoot, he'll be in a class by himself. Macauley, a great shooter and competitor, was too frail to grab rebounds off the backboards. Russell turned out to be one of the best rebound men in the league, and before he's through, he's likely to set a few records in that department.

Red outsmarted the whole league when he got Frank Ramsey, one of the greatest competitors I have ever seen. The N.B.A. had set up a temporary rule which happened to apply to the University of Kentucky, where Ramsey went. Red found a loophole in the rule which permitted him to grab not only Ramsey but Cliff Hagan and Lou Tsioropoulos, two of his teammates at Kentucky. The rule was changed, but the Celtics kept all three.

Despite his crack about local yokels, Auerbach didn't care where a good basketball player came from. So when Tom Heinsohn got out of Holy Cross, Red told Walter to grab him. Heinsohn, another great competitor, was a top man on our championship team of 1957.

Auerbach is a great coach because he knows how to put the right team together—one of the big problems for a pro coach—and what tactics to use. The tactics employed by the Celtics have resulted in the highest scoring in all basketball history.

Auerbach likes a fast-breaking team that can recover and get the ball down the court before the opposing team knows what's happening. In order to do that, you must have a per-fectly-conditioned team. It takes an astonishing amount of energy to operate the way the Celtics do. When the N.B.A. season begins, we are in top condition because Auerbach has us running in practice sessions until our tongues are hanging out.

Red is strictly a percentage player. He goes with his best no matter what is happening on the court. In the final play-off game with St. Louis in 1957, both Sharman and I were cold. Neither one of us was hitting. But Red kept us in for almost the entire game, which was a long one that went into two overtimes.

"Why did he keep Sharman and Cousy in when they were going so poorly?" roared Red's critics.

"Because they are ordinarily my best shooters," Red replied. "They figured to hit sooner or later. But they're not going to hit sitting on the bench so I kept them in."

It didn't work out that way, but Red was right. If either of us had gotten hot, we'd have won the game in regulation time. One of us figured to get hot so in my book Red was right leaving us in.

○

Scoring baskets is much like getting base hits in baseball. When a ballplayer goes into a slump at the plate, he has his own formula for pulling himself out of it. Some guys just try to meet the ball. Others change their batting stance. Still others decide to hit only certain types of pitches. There are as many cures for slumps as there are ballplayers.

The same thing is true in basketball. When you can't dunk those shots in, you're in a slump and must do what you can to pull out of it. If I'm having a bad night, I have a few rules of my own which I follow. The main thing is to keep on shooting. This is easy under a coach like Red, who leaves his top men in even if they are going badly. As he points out, you can't score from the bench. But I try to pick my shots so that when I take them, I have the best possible chance of scoring.

For example, when I'm in a slump, I never try a radical shot like a left-handed hook or a thirty-foot set shot. I'm going to work for the easiest shot in the book, the layup. I work hard to get in so close that if I have a shot, it will be one I can't miss. If I get in a couple of layups, my confidence returns and I start hitting again. Naturally, it doesn't always happen that way, but it happens often enough so that I find it worth while to try. When I'm hot, I can hit with all kinds of shots from all kinds of angles. But when I'm cold, I can't hit with much of anything until I get back into my groove.

One of the big differences between a baseball slump and a basketball slump is that a baseball slump can last for weeks, but a basketball slump rarely lasts more than a night. Sometimes you can pull out of a slump before a game is over. In any event, you can usually pull out before you play another game. A prolonged slump by a normally good shooter is a rare thing in basketball.

Of course, a basketball player has more control over a slump than a baseball player. If a baseball player is facing a hot pitcher, his chances of breaking the slump that day aren't very good. But a basketball player has only himself to fight. If he keeps his head and doesn't make it too much of a fight, he can pull out of his slump through his own efforts, regardless of the opposition.

☉

When I first joined the Celtics in 1950, the club had been struggling through a maze of ghastly financial losses for four years. It was originally formed as a Boston Garden Corporation promotion, but the Garden directors finally gave up on it. Walter Brown, the Garden's managing director, who was also president of the Boston Bruins hockey team, took over the Celtics as a personal venture. His partner was and still is Lou Pieri of Providence, Rhode Island. Pieri, owner of the Rhode Island Auditorium, once played basketball and knew the game well. But Brown, an ice hockey enthusiast, didn't know a basketball from a watermelon when he first got involved in the Celtics.

All Walter knew was that he liked to watch basketball. And he figured that if a college team could jam the Garden the way Holy Cross did, a professional team could do even better. The Garden people went into basketball on Brown's recommendation and dropped the Celtics over Brown's protests.

Brown's faith in a game about which he knew so little has finally paid off handsomely, but he lost his shirt before the Celtics began making money in 1954. At one point, he had hocked about everything he owned for the ball club, including his personal reputation as a sports promoter. Everyone around him except the basketball people was urging him to get out before the Celtics ruined him altogether. They tell me Pieri even offered to buy him out for the purpose of junking the club (Pieri had had to junk his own Providence Steamrollers because they couldn't make money), and Walter steadfastly refused. He was absolutely certain that sooner or later the Celtics would become a big thing in Boston.

But the years went on, and the Celtics kept losing money while Walter went deeper and deeper into the hole. Patient as he was, he couldn't help but blow his stack once in a while. He needed some sort of escape valve, and it had to be the Celtics. It was as sure as death and taxes that Walter Brown would hit the ceiling half a dozen times a season—and he did.

Brown, a broad-shouldered, sandy-haired, blue-eyed Irishman, has a quick temper and a big heart. He can get mad faster and cool off cooler than any man I've ever seen. When he gets hot under the collar, the whole world knows it, particularly when he does it at press luncheons in Boston. But give him a night's sleep, and he wakes up ready to apologize for everything.

In my book, Brown shouldn't be classified as a promoter at all. He's too nice a guy, too honest, too anxious to do the right thing. He's one of the great humanitarians of my acquaintance. He has given generously of his time and money to all sorts of charitable causes. He is known throughout New England for his work with the Jimmy Fund, which raises money for research in children's cancer, and with the Variety Club, which started the Jimmy Fund.

Walter's word is his bond. A handshake with him is as good as a signed contract. But both he and Red Auerbach are apt to say more than they mean when something bothers them. For years the Garden has run basketball luncheons for the Boston press. Things might have been pretty quiet on the basketball court, but they were always jumping at the press luncheons. Between Walter's flareups and Red's press-baiting there was always something doing. The Celtics didn't win, but boy, did they have fireworks!

Through no particular fault of my own, I was occasionally in the middle of these rhubarbs. I didn't even have to be at the luncheon to find myself in hot water. Within a couple of years after I joined the club, I was its highest-paid player. Right behind me, and in high brackets, were Ed Macauley and Bill Sharman. Brown paid the three of us almost as much as some other teams were getting. And if I'm not mistaken, shortly after George Mikan retired in 1955 we were the top three men in the league.

Brown had no objection to paying us all that money. In fact, he was very generous about raises, especially in my case. But when he was mad at the club, he took it out on its highest-paid members. Sometimes he blasted the whole team at once and sometimes only a few of us, but when he got down to one, it was usually Cousy.

Naturally the sports writers had a Roman holiday whenever this happened and Walter or Red was involved. They faithfully reported every word that was uttered so even though I was not often present at the lunches, I had no trouble finding out what happened.

I got more laughs than tears out of these outbursts and so did Walter when he cooled off enough to think about them. One of his funniest cracks came a few years ago when he got up at a luncheon after we'd lost a bad game. He talked about the game, then said ominously, "There are going to be some changes around here. I don't need an expensive club to lose games. I can lose just as easily with a cheap one."

When I first joined the team, I began commuting to Boston from Worcester, about thirty-five miles away. Neither Red nor Walter said anything to me about it, but the newspapers kept reporting that both were anxious for me to live in town during the season. They were afraid I'd get into an auto accident or something and be late to a game. But I usually allowed enough time so that I could make it easily even if some unavoidable delay came up.

One night I had a flat tire, and, of course, that was the night I hadn't allowed enough time. I was late leaving Worcester, and I knew if I stopped to change the tire, I'd miss part of the game. Some friends of mine came along and picked me up, but they didn't get me to the Garden on time. The game started just as I walked into the locker room, and I didn't get to the floor until the first quarter was well under way.

We all had a bad night and lost to Syracuse. And when the game was over, Walter was quoted as saying to the writers, "It was all Cousy's fault. If he'd gotten here on time, we might have won. He's going to move to Boston tomorrow."

Someone grabbed me before I left, told me what Walter

was supposed to have said and asked, "Are you moving in town tomorrow?"

"Wait until tomorrow," I said. Then I went home.

The next day Walter said, "It wasn't Cousy's fault we lost the game. It was mine. I had the basketball floor laid out north-to-south at the Garden instead of east-to-west, the way it usually is. I wanted to experiment with possible new seating arrangements. But the switch hurt our guys. It was just as if they were playing on a strange court. They lost the advantage a team usually gets when it plays at home."

Incidentally, a week or so after I showed up late at that Syracuse game, somebody sent me a set of blowout-proof tire tubes. I thought it was a pretty good gag.

Walter never did ask me to move to Boston. As a matter of fact, while Missie and I were waiting to get into a new house we had purchased in Worcester the following autumn, Walter turned his summer home on Cape Cod over to us so my family would have a place to stay.

Maybe there was method in his madness at that. While Missie stayed in Walter's house, I lived in a Boston apartment with a couple of other guys on the team.

Auerbach touched off a rhubarb one day when he was reported to have torn Macauley, Sharman and me apart. This was at a press luncheon in December of 1953 after the Celtics had played a particularly lousy game in losing to the Philadelphia Warriors. Even then, I wouldn't have been bothered if I had known all the facts, which I didn't.

On the afternoon before the luncheon I think I scored four points in a game that was studded with rhubarbs. There were a dozen arguments and one open fight. I got slightly hurt, although not badly enough to have to leave the game for any length of time. My injury, such as it was, didn't account for my bad shooting either. It was just one of those days.

I didn't attend the luncheon, and I didn't hear anything

about what happened there until I got home for dinner that night. There was a string of messages for me to call Boston and Worcester sports writers. Before I had a chance to start calling, the phone rang. It was a Boston reporter.

"Did you hear what Red said about you at the luncheon today?" the guy asked.

"No," I said.

"Well, he was pretty rough."

"Why shouldn't he be?" I said. "We stunk the house out yesterday."

"He said you weren't shooting enough," the writer said.

"Is that so?" I answered vaguely. I was mildly annoyed, not so much at what he might have said as what he would be quoted as saying.

"And when Red got through," the writer said, "Walter also had a few choice remarks."

"Is that so?" I commented again. And I began to burn. For a minute I forgot I was talking to a newspaperman, forgot that Walter always cools off on a night's sleep and that Red always talks over things like that with me. All I could think of was that whenever things went wrong with the ball club, I always seemed to be the goat.

"What do you think about all this?" the writer asked.

"I don't know what to think," I said. "I'm confused."

Then I had the brains to say good-bye and hang up.

But before I could think things out the phone rang again, and it rang for the next few hours. The more people talked to me, the more upset I got. Now there were rumors that Walter wanted to trade me, and what did I think of that?

I didn't know what to think. All I know is I got finessed into talking about which other teams in the league, if any, would pick up my salary if the Celtics did put me on the market.

And pretty soon I realized I'd have to do something about it before I went crazy.

So between calls I managed to get in a few words with Joe Sharry.

"Get me on Tom Decker's show," I said. "I might as well let everybody know what I'm thinking."

Tom Decker was a sports announcer on a Worcester radio station. Everyone in town who had any interest in sports listened to him, and I figured that maybe the phone would stop ringing if I told his audience what was on my mind.

"I don't understand this trade talk," I said on the air. "I'm pretty upset about it. I don't understand why these statements about me were made at the luncheon in Boston today. If the Celtics aren't satisfied with my playing, I want to be traded."

Then the fat was in the fire. Instead of shutting the phone off, that crack set it ringing faster than ever. Everyone and his brother-in-law had the same question: "Is it true you want to be traded?"

I finally got to bed, but I didn't get much sleep. I was worried about Walter and Red wanting to deal me off and sore at myself for making such a foolish remark. I kept thinking how happy I was when I first joined the Celtics, and the more I thought about it, the more I kicked myself for talking as if I wanted to leave.

Yet I was still mad at Walter and Red. If they'd said all the things people told me they'd said, the least they could have done would have been to give me a little advance notice instead of bleating everything out at a press luncheon.

We were playing in Minneapolis the next night, but instead of meeting the team in Boston, I got a flight west directly out of Worcester. I wanted to be alone in a place where I could think some more. The thinking I did wasn't very helpful. I still had no idea where I stood with the Celtics by the time I landed in Minneapolis.

But a couple of hours after I arrived, Red called me in my hotel room.

"Can I come up?" he said. "I want to talk to you."

"I can't wait," I said. "Don't spare the horses."

A couple of minutes later he was there.

"Lot of excitement yesterday," he remarked.

"I'll say," I said.

Then he said, "Look, nobody wants to trade you. Get that straight."

"Got it," I said. "As a matter of fact, I don't want to go anywhere. If the Celtics traded me, I'd quit this game."

We talked for a couple of hours, and he explained everything. He told me he hadn't made any such statements as had been quoted and that what he had said had all been magnified in the paper. He told me that neither he nor Walter had said a word about trading me. And he told me a lot of other things, all of which satisfied me completely.

Later, after I got home, I saw the Boston papers for the day we'd left. They all quoted Walter as being sorry, and one even quoted him as saying, "The first thing we've got to do is square ourselves with Cousy."

I don't know whether he said that or not, but it wasn't necessary. The minute I had it straight from Red, there was nothing to square.

16 | *A dream come true*

I AM NO HOLIER-THAN-THOU CRUSADING KNIGHT IN SHINING armor, fighting for the rights of the common man. I have no axes to grind with Capital, nor do I consider myself a champion of Labor. I have no unusually noble motives, nor do I want to be painted as a great emancipator of struggling professional basketball players. All I've ever asked for myself and the boys in our business is a fair shake. Which is why I formed a players' union, officially known as the N.B.A. Players' Association.

I got the idea of a players' union in 1953. I had always felt that there was a need for something that would give the players a voice in the operation of the league's affairs. We had a big stake in pro basketball—almost as big as the owners'. If the league folded, eighty specialists would be thrown out of jobs. We should have something to say in the protection of those jobs.

Practically all of us were college graduates with a fair degree of intelligence. Some of the guys had some pretty good ideas, but without a union, they had no way of expressing

155

themselves. Maurice Podoloff, the N.B.A. president, was pretty busy trying to keep the loose ends from falling apart. He didn't have much time to listen to player gripes.

Back in '53 the league was struggling for its very existence. It's strong today and getting stronger because the pro game is much better established than it was in '53. But at the time, we knew that if we were going to have a real big league, the bush league stuff would have to go.

I had no desire to form a red-eyed union, complete with demands for higher pay, shorter hours, longer vacations and elaborate pension setups. But I had been listening to player gripes and making a few of my own for nearly four years, and I had a pretty good idea of what improvements should be made.

I had had no experience with unions and had never belonged to one. I had a very fuzzy idea of what should be done to form one and was also skeptical as to how some of the players, to say nothing of the owners, would react to the idea. But I was sure that most of the players would go along with me.

I talked to as many as I could during the 1953-54 season in order to sound out personal opinions. Every time I heard a gripe, I brought up the union idea just to see how the griper took to it.

For example, a player on a western club remarked one night, "I'm dished! We had an exhibition game last night after six league games in six nights. How the heck can they expect us to stay in shape?"

"They can't," I said. "That's why we need a union. Maybe we can control the exhibition games."

I also thought the players should have some say about the regular schedule. Sometimes it looked as if the guy who made it up took lessons from the Marquis de Sade. There were schedule quirks that were positively diabolic.

For example, here was a typical week for us:

One Saturday we flew by chartered plane from Boston to Rochester, New York, for a night game with the Royals. As soon as it was over, we got back into the plane and started an all-night flight to Minneapolis. We arrived there Sunday morning about eight o'clock. By the time we got to the hotel, it was nearer nine. We fell into bed for a snappy three hours' sleep because we had to play the Lakers at two o'clock in the afternoon.

Don't ask me what would have happened if the plane had broken down or if we had been grounded somewhere. It would have been impossible to schedule a night game in Rochester and an afternoon game the next day in Minneapolis without depending entirely on a chartered plane.

We spent Sunday night in Minneapolis and flew to Milwaukee Monday morning. We had that night off—the only idle night of the entire trip. We played the Hawks Tuesday night, then flew to St. Louis the next morning. We played the Hawks there again Wednesday night and flew to Fort Wayne Thursday morning. After a game with the Pistons Thursday night, we had another all-night flight to Boston, arriving home Friday morning. And that night we played in the Boston Garden.

If this had been an emergency arrangement to get some postponements out of the way or something like that, nobody would have given it a second thought. But this was a *typical* week not only for the Celtics but for everyone else in the league. All winter long, professional basketball players were criss-crossing the eastern part of the country like flies. And that's the way it had been every winter.

A certain amount of running around is essential in our business. I'm one of the most frantic travelers of all since I'm on the road with exhibition tours and special operations ten months of the year. Even during the summer months I have to leave my camp from time to time in the interests of the business. Other guys are in the same boat.

But with intelligent scheduling, all the necessary league games could be played with a minimum of travel. All the boys agree that we have to play one-night stands. Unlike baseball teams, which can schedule games in series, basketball teams have to share indoor arenas with hockey games, ice shows, track meets, fights and all sorts of special events.

We had other gripes, including senseless and exorbitant fines. The referees need some sort of weapon to keep games under control. None of us thought that the league would eliminate fines altogether. But we did expect fair treatment, and many of the guys felt that they weren't getting it. This was a particular gripe of mine. My first six years in the league cost me several hundred bucks a year in fines. In 1956-57, I made up my mind I wouldn't pay the front office another dime. I kept my head all season and went through the entire year without drawing a single fine.

During the period when I was trying to figure out how to form a union, I collected gripes wherever I went. One thing that bothered me a lot was the league president's partiality to certain players, coaches, and owners. For example, he often ignored the coaches' rating of referees. The Celtics invariably drew someone they didn't want for big games.

Some players, coaches, and owners can do no wrong in Podoloff's eyes; others can get away with murder. Yet Red Auerbach couldn't flick a cigar ash without paying through the nose for it. Red probably gave up more money in fines than any other coach in the business. He's a bleeder during a ball game, and he sometimes loses his head completely. But Podoloff always seemed to take it for granted that Red was wrong in a rhubarb. Red still gets fined faster and heavier than anyone else in the league.

This was the sort of thing I wanted to square away when I figured out my union plans. We had no weapon of retaliation in cases of unfair treatment by Podoloff or anyone else. Since I was one of the highest paid men in the league, I felt that it was up to me to form a union. An organization of low-paid players would be useless, and if it didn't have the top men, it couldn't live very long.

I talked the situation over with Joe Sharry during the off-season, and he advised me to go ahead and sound out players on other clubs. I had already polled the Celtics, and I knew they were all for a union. But now I wanted more specific information. So during the summer of 1954, I wrote to eight players, each representing a different team in the league. I tried to pick men who were top ballplayers, guys who wouldn't be badly hurt when it was revealed that they were pioneers in a basketball union movement. And in each letter I asked the man to poll his teammates for their opinion as well.

I wrote to Don Sunderlage, a guard for the Milwaukee Hawks and his team's high scorer the previous season; Dolph Schayes of the Syracuse Nats, his team's top scorer in 1953-54 and one of the great all-time players; Carl Braun of the New York Knicks, who had led his team in scoring that year; Jim Pollard of the Minneapolis Lakers, second to George Mikan in scoring (I didn't contact Mikan because I knew he was preparing to retire, and I wasn't sure he'd be interested); Bobby Davies, a top player for the Rochester Royals; Paul Arizin, a Philadelphia Warriors' standout; Paul Hoffman of the

Baltimore Bullets (which folded soon after the 1954-55 season got under way) and Andy Phillip, a Fort Wayne star who is now with the Celtics.

Basketball players are notoriously bad letter-writers. Maybe it's because they travel so much they figure that sooner or later they'll run into a would-be correspondent. I sent the letters out in mid-summer of 1954 and hoped I'd have answers by the time the season began in mid-autumn. Within three weeks I had replies from all but Phillip. Every single man said he was vitally interested in forming a union, and they all thought they were expressing the opinion of the majority of guys on their clubs. Some were even certain that the feeling was unanimous.

I didn't find out why Phillip hadn't replied until I saw him after the season began.

"Did you get my letter?" I asked him.

"Yes," he said. "I didn't write because I knew I'd see you."

"How do you guys feel about the union?"

"I put it up to the boys," Andy said, "and they decided against it."

"Why?" I asked.

Andy looked at me a moment, then said, "Why do *you* think?"

He didn't have to say any more. I knew right away what he meant. The Pistons were afraid of what their owner, Fred Zollner, would do if they went in with us.

Zollner, a wealthy Fort Wayne industrialist, was the league's only financial giant. He was a great basketball fan, and his club was his hobby. He often had his boys flown around the country in his private plane, and he treated them all very well.

The league was so weak at the time that it needed Zollner far worse than Zollner needed it. If Zollner had decided to pull out, it would have been a terrible blow to the N.B.A. His

players were well aware of this fact. And because he had often
expressed himself as being dead set against unions in general,
they didn't dare come into the Players' Association.

At the 1955 All-Star game in New York I went to Zollner
and asked, "Do you object to your ballplayers joining our
union?"

"I certainly do," he replied.

"Don't you think they should have something to say about
how the league is run?" I asked.

"They can say it without forming a union," he answered.

"Every team in the league except the Pistons wants a union,"
I explained. "Your guys are holding up the whole works."

"Look," he said. "I've never had a union in my shops, and
I won't have a union on my ball club. If any of my people
have a grievance, they know they can tell me about it, and
we'll get it unraveled. And the same thing goes for my basketball team. Those boys know how much I like them, and I'll
always be sympathetic to their problems. They don't need a
union, and they know it."

This was a fine kettle of fish. It was like the New York department stores trying to get a union going without Macy's.
Fort Wayne might have been a comparatively small town
(the Pistons have since moved to Detroit) but because of
Zollner's financial position, its club was vitally important to the
N.B.A. We couldn't afford to antagonize Zollner. If he were to
withdraw his team, the league might be set back ten years. We
didn't dare press demands for the Pistons to join the union.

So for the next couple of years we had to go ahead without Fort Wayne. We had no choice. It was either that or no
union at all.

In the meantime, both Joe Sharry and I had talked to
major league baseball players we knew about their players'
association, which is highly successful. These boys were

very cooperative and gave us plenty of valuable tips. Through one of them we met C. Keefe (Connie) Hurley, a Boston attorney who had once been a baseball player and was familiar with some of the problems of professional athletes. Hurley agreed to handle our affairs for nothing until we were established.

I wrote another letter to the eight players I had previously contacted, asking them to supervise the election of official player representatives from their teams. When this was done, we decided to have an organizational meeting at the All-Star game in New York in January, 1955. Every team except Baltimore, which had folded, and Fort Wayne was represented at that meeting. Joe Sharry also attended and agreed to become secretary-treasurer of the Association. Hurley was unable to be there, but he came to all our subsequent meetings.

We talked at great length about what we wanted and what we should ask for. We couldn't make our demands too stiff because of the shaky financial condition of some of the teams in the league. We had to be careful to ask for just those things that were absolutely essential.

Much as we wanted to request some kind of minimum salary deal, we knew it was impossible at the time. While some clubs could have afforded it, such a demand might drive others right out of the league. For the same reason, we couldn't mention anything about a pension plan. That too would have to wait until the teams were stronger in the pocketbook.

We would have liked to mention something about the regular league schedules, but there again we had to be careful. Basketball was the Johnny-come-lately of professional winter sports. Those sports that had been well established before the N.B.A. was in existence had first choice on the big arena dates, and for the most part we had to take the leavings. We knew that if we squawked too much about playing dates, we might upset the whole applecart.

After an all-day session, we finally decided on a set of five basic requests to be presented to the president. These "demands" would have put a mouse to shame. All five were hardly more than a basketball player's bill of rights. They were all points that should have been handled by the league in the natural course of events.

Here they were:

1. *Payment of salaries to the members of the defunct Baltimore club.* This was basic. The Bullets folded too early to handle their salary obligations and too late for the majority of the boys to make other connections. When the front office defaulted on salaries, we took it as a perfect matter of course that the league would pay the boys off. But weeks and months went by, and nothing happened.

I finally went to see Podoloff myself, asking him in the name of fairness to take care of these guys. He put me off then on the ground that it wasn't the league's responsibility. However, the boys were finally paid by the league, but only after we had submitted our five demands to Podoloff's office in writing. By then all the guys were well established in new jobs, and while they were glad to get the money, they weren't desperately in need of it as some were at the time the club collapsed.

2. *Establishment of a twenty-game limit on exhibition games, after which the players should share in the profits.*

The unreasonable number of exhibition games, particularly in mid-season, was a big headache to some teams and no headache at all to others. Since I've been with the Celtics, for example, they've never played as many as twenty in a season and neither have the Knickerbockers. But so many other guys had gripes on this subject that we felt it should be included.

Too many exhibition games were bound to hurt the league. A tired ballplayer can't give his best, and the customer who pays the freight is entitled to nothing less than that. Some owners treated their players like chattels, moving them around the country at will for useless exhibition games which benefited nobody but the guy who picked up the check.

In any event, if an owner insisted on playing more than twenty games, we felt that the players who did all the heavy work should be paid extra money. As it was, they didn't get a dime over their regular salary, no matter how many exhibition games they played.

3. *Abolition of the so-called "whispering fine."*

This was a universal gripe throughout the league. The "whispering fine" was an invention of the devil. No other sport had such a thing, and I cannot conceive of any other sport establishing one. I never discovered who thought up this mad device which was a mean, unhealthy form of referee dictatorship that left a player helpless to defend himself.

When an official calls a technical foul on a man, the result is an automatic fine of $25. The foul is called openly, and everyone knows at once who it is on and why. But someone dreamed up the idea of the "whispering fine" as a means of punishment for a rule infraction too serious to be ignored but not serious enough to warrant a technical foul call.

The "whispering fine" was really a nasty little secret between the official and the player. When the player did something wrong, the referee ran over and whispered, "That'll cost you ten bucks"—or whatever he thought the infraction was worth. There was no foul shot penalty and no announcement that the fine had been levied.

Usually there weren't even any witnesses. In the case of a dispute, it was only the player's word against the referee's. Obviously, the player never had a chance. We didn't object to the size of the fine or the setting up of a penalty to cover the situation. All we objected to was the way it was called.

4. *Payment of $25 expenses for public appearances other than radio, television or certain charitable functions.*

In view of the huge payoffs that some athletes get for public appearances, including radio and television, this was certainly a modest demand on our part. In the early days of the league, ballplayers would go practically anywhere to speak because they had to sell both the league and basketball, particularly in a city like Boston. Even today, N.B.A. players are glad to help promote the game in any way they can. But in some cases people had taken advantage of the boys, which was why we included this point in our original demands.

5. *Establishment of an impartial board of arbitration to settle player-owner disputes.*

This could hardly be called a rabble-rouser of an issue. Actually, it was as much to the owners' advantage as the players' to have such a board. In cases where the player was obviously wrong, a fair-minded player-observer would vote with the owners. This would happen, in effect, when a boy fresh out of college held out for an unreasonable salary. He would call me and ask me what he should do. I would investigate the situation, then call him back after a meeting of players and tell him we couldn't back him on his demands.

○

We presented the five demands in writing to Maurice Podoloff shortly after the 1955 All-Star game. He ignored them for several weeks. Then I went to see him.

"Aren't you going to do anything?" I asked after we had talked a few minutes.

"Everything will be taken care of," he said.

"When?" I asked.

He gave me an evasive answer, and I couldn't pin him down to any commitments. He agreed that the Baltimore players should be paid, but he wouldn't tell me when or how they'd collect. And he neither agreed nor disagreed on any of the other points.

It was a highly unsatisfactory interview, and I walked out of his office mad. From time to time, we had subsequent talks which were just as unsatisfactory. Podoloff, a friendly guy under most circumstances, was obviously as much against the union as I was for it. He resented me for forming it, and he showed less and less interest in it. He got pretty sick of me too. In his eyes I was a prime trouble-maker, a rabble-rouser trying to fire up a bunch of happy ballplayers into rebellion.

As a firer-upper, I was a flop. When time passed and nothing happened, the boys showed less and less interest in the union. About a year after the Bullets folded, the Baltimore boys got their money, but that was the only demand we'd made that the league paid any attention to. The "whispering fines" remained in effect, exhibition games were unlimited, no provision was made for paying players for public appearances, and nothing was done to give the players a say in arbitrating player-owner disputes.

Instead of gaining ground, we lost it. We had meetings at the 1956 and 1957 All-Star games, but while everyone attended, only a handful took part in the proceedings. We seemed to be on a treadmill.

One day before the 1957 meeting, I asked Joe Sharry to investigate the possibilities of our joining an established union. He checked with someone in the American Federation of Labor but was referred to A.G.F.A., the actors' union. An A.G.F.A. representative, Jack Bright, agreed to come to our

1957 meeting at the All-Star game in Boston and give us a rundown on his organization.

Immediately after the All-Star game luncheon at the Garden and just before our meeting with Bright, Maurice Podoloff asked over the Garden loudspeaker if the player representatives would meet him in the Garden Club, adjoining the offices. When we got there, Podoloff told us that the owners were having a meeting in St. Louis on April 18 and would like to have us present. We accepted the invitation.

We didn't know if this meant action or not. We went ahead with our meeting with Bright, but I think it might have scared some of the players. While they were perfectly willing to go along with the idea of a Players' Association, they didn't like the possibility of affiliating with an outside organization. I must admit I wasn't crazy about that part of it either, but we weren't getting any action by ourselves, and I couldn't figure out any alternative.

Dolph Schayes, the Syracuse representative, and I were slated for an exhibition basketball tour in the west by April 18, but Schayes agreed to go back to St. Louis with me to attend the meeting. Ed Macauley, the St. Louis Hawks' representative, also promised to go. So did Harry Gallatin of the New York Knickerbockers. Connie Hurley, our lawyer, was also scheduled to attend.

I didn't have much hope that we'd get anything done. It figured to be the same old brushoff. Podoloff had shown no more interest in our affairs than before, and I couldn't believe that he had any intention of helping us. Frankly, I was discouraged and getting tired of the whole business. I still wanted to see something accomplished, but except for a few scattered and dedicated ballplayers, nobody else seemed to care.

Just before the close of the regular season, cards went out to the player representatives which were to be signed by the members of all teams and returned to Joe Sharry along with a year's dues. We wanted to get the cards back quickly, and it was easy for each representative to round up the boys while they were all together.

Fort Wayne was still out of the Association and nothing came in from the Philadelphia Warriors or the Rochester (now Cincinnati) Royals, but we heard from most of the others on schedule. The playoffs began, and we still didn't hear anything. Then just after the Warriors were eliminated, I got a letter from their representative, Neil Johnston. He enclosed his personal check for dues but nothing else.

"I want to remain a member of the Association in good standing," he wrote, in part, "but the other fellows have decided to pull out."

I couldn't believe my eyes. I tried to reach Neil, but he had gone home, and I couldn't contact him. I tried to reach other guys on the Philadelphia club, but they were also unavailable.

While I was still trying to dope out what to do next, I got a letter from Richie Regan, the Royals' representative. He told me that the team had broken up so quickly after being eliminated from the playoffs that he hadn't had time to get the cards signed or collect dues. And because of his wife's illness he had had to rush home.

"The hell with this," I told Joe Sharry. "I'm getting out."

He agreed with me. I'd beaten my brains out for nearly three years trying to get something going that nobody seemed to want. I'd spent long hours getting myself in wrong with the president of the league fighting for things that couldn't help me much anyhow. I was getting more money than anyone else in the league, I was working for the fairest owner in the business and I had nothing to gain from a union.

Those were my first thoughts. Then as I began figuring things out, I decided that if I got out, perhaps it would wake the boys up. I couldn't fire them up by fighting for them. Maybe if I stopped fighting, it would have the right effect.

I phoned Howie McHugh, the Celtics' publicity director, and asked him to call a press conference for me at the Boston Garden. We were waiting for the result of the Minneapolis-St. Louis playoffs in the west to find out which team we'd play in the finals so the pressure on us wasn't as great. This seemed as good a time as any for me to announce I was through with the Association.

But before McHugh could arrange the press conference I'd requested, I heard from Joe Sharry.

"I just talked to Ed Macauley in St. Louis," Joe said. "He wants you to stay in—at least until that April 18 meeting of the owners."

"They won't do anything," I said. "What's the use?"

"Maybe they will," said Joe. "Macauley thinks it's ridiculous to throw in the towel now after you've been fighting all this time."

"What do you think?" I asked.

"I'm beginning to think he's right."

"Let's call Hurley," I suggested.

So we called Connie Hurley, our lawyer. Like Macauley, he was violently opposed to my getting out at that time.

"Wait until the St. Louis meeting," he said. "It's only a few weeks away. If nothing happens then, you can get out. But if you quit now, it will do more harm than good."

I was convinced. I told McHugh to forget the press conference. And while we played the long, exciting final series with the Hawks for the title, which we won, I temporarily forgot the Association.

But after the series was over, I didn't have time to think of much else. The playoffs ended on Saturday, April 13, in Boston. On Sunday, the 14th, we left for an exhibition tour between the Celtics and a team of N.B.A. all-stars. We played the first game of that tour in Des Moines on Monday, the 15th. On Tuesday, the 16th, we were in Denver, and we played in Provo, Utah, on the 17th. On the 18th, we were scheduled to play in Salt Lake City with Spokane on the schedule for the 19th.

Schayes played on the all-star team that opposed us. We checked plane schedules and figured out that by traveling all night on the 17th and all afternoon on the 18th, we could make the St. Louis meeting and still not miss any of the games.

With good weather we could have done it, but we didn't get good weather. The result was the weirdest wild goose chase I've ever known. We started this daffy argosy after the game in Provo on the night of the 17th. We were able to get a night flight out of Salt Lake City which would get us to St. Louis at 8:30 in the morning. And according to our schedule, we could leave St. Louis at 2:30 in the afternoon and get back to Salt Lake in time for the game there.

We got a ride from Provo to Salt Lake and made the plane easily. It was the last thing that came easily for the next thirty-six hours.

We took off from Salt Lake on schedule, and Dolph and I settled back for a few hours' sleep. I slept fitfully, waking up from time to time, though never completely asleep or awake. At seven or so in the morning I looked out the window but couldn't see a thing. We were in the midst of a pea-soup fog.

I asked the stewardess how we were doing.

"Not so hot," she said. "It looks like we're not going to get into St. Louis."

I sat up straight and asked the standard question: "Socked in?"

She nodded.

"What happens to us then?"

"We hope we can get into Chicago," she said, "but right now that's fogged in too."

"And if we don't make Chicago?" I asked in a small voice. She shrugged.

"The whole Middle West is fogged in."

I tried to sleep but couldn't. I tried to read and couldn't do that either. We didn't get into Chicago so we headed for Cleveland.

"It doesn't look good," the stewardess said, "but it may open up."

"What's after Cleveland?" I asked her.

"Boston," she said.

"Ouch! That's where I came in!"

But we made Cleveland. We landed there just in time to get on a plane headed for St. Louis. Schayes stayed awake long enough to walk from one plane to the other, then promptly went back to sleep.

We were delayed in getting out of Cleveland but finally took off. We landed in St. Louis at 1:15 P.M.

"That gives us maybe an hour," said Dolph. "Not enough time to go into town."

"We'll have to call up," I said.

I got hold of Macauley at the hotel.

"It looks good," Ed said.

"It does?"

"Everyone is being very nice," he told me. "I think we're going to make some progress."

"Do you need us?" I asked.

"We'll be all right, I think. Go on back to Salt Lake," he said.

When I hung up, Dolph suddenly yelled, "Hey, they're calling our flight!"

"It's only 1:30," I said.

But we rushed to our counter, and sure enough, it was our flight going out. We'd made a one-hour miscalculation on the St. Louis-Salt Lake flight. Instead of leaving St. Louis at 2:30, it was going at 1:30.

We barely made it.

"Nice town, St. Louis," Schayes commented.

"Yeah," I said. "They have such comfortable phone booths."

"You ought to know," he said. "That's all you saw there."

"You didn't even see that," I replied.

Our first stop was Kansas City. It turned out to be our last. Everything west of there was socked in.

We tried every air line we'd ever heard of and half a dozen we didn't know existed. No one would take us any farther. By five in the afternoon, we gave up. I had to phone the boys at Salt Lake City and tell them we'd miss the game. We arranged to meet the gang at Spokane.

But getting to Spokane, even with twenty-four hours' notice, wasn't so easy, at least from Kansas City. We couldn't get into Denver, the big transfer point, and nobody knew exactly what we should do. We were just beginning to consider train schedules to see if we could get part way at least when we ran into Johnny Kundla, then the coach and now the general manager of the Minneapolis Lakers.

We told him our troubles, and he unraveled them with one quick stroke of genius.

"Come on to Minneapolis with me," he said. "Planes from there to Spokane come a dime a dozen."

So we went to Minneapolis.

We spent a couple of hours in the Minneapolis air-port, then got a plane to Spokane at about three in the morn-ing. So we were in the air for the second straight night. I don't think I slept a wink. I didn't have to because Schayes was mak-ing up for both of us.

When we landed in Spokane, I didn't even stop to buy a paper. I crawled into a cab, went to the hotel and fell into bed for the first time in about fifty hours.

Two hours later I got a phone call to go on the air for the good of the game. On the way out I bought a paper. And there on the sports page was a small item that made my spine tingle.

"St. Louis, April 18 (AP):" I read. "The National Basket-ball Association board of governors, for the first time, granted formal recognition Thursday to the N.B.A. Players' Associa-tion and agreed to meet annually with player representatives.

"Ed Macauley of the St. Louis Hawks, acting as spokesman for the player representatives, said, 'We believe the players will be happy with this.' "

○

Happy! I was almost hysterical! That crazy trip had cost me two nights' sleep and three hundred dollars of my own money, and I hadn't accomplished a thing, but I didn't regret a minute or a dime.

As soon as I could get to a phone, I called Macauley. He gave me a brief rundown on the meeting and its results.

"They okayed practically everything," he said.

I couldn't wait to write Missie:

The results of that meeting made it all worth while. It's taken three long years, and I don't think I've ever received a greater thrill or felt more personal satisfaction than I do at this moment. I'm only sorry I can't share it with you.

By the time you receive this letter, you will know that the owners granted the majority of our requests along with a promise to meet with us each year with transportation costs to be paid by them.

You can't imagine how glad I am that I didn't throw in the towel last month after Philadelphia and Rochester dropped out.

Several days later Missie forwarded a letter from Connie Hurley along with a copy of the agreement between the owners and the players. The letter, which is one of my proudest possessions, reads as follows:

"Dear Bob:

I am enclosing herewith a photo copy of the instrument of agreement which Maurice Podoloff signed on behalf of the Board of Governors last Thursday, April 18, 1957, at St. Louis. This is for your own personal files, as I have already sent the original to Joe Sharry to be kept in the files of the Association.

I feel that you should take warranted pride in the accomplishment exemplified by the within agreement. I am sure that it is ninety-nine per cent due to your own individual stick-to-itiveness. At least it represents a personal triumph on your part over the President, Mr. Podoloff, which is incidental by comparison with the beneficial results to the players as a body.

Sincerely yours,
C. Keefe Hurley.

The agreement gave us practically everything we'd asked for and then some. Here's what it said in part:

The Board of Governors of the National Basketball Association, in annual meeting assembled, hereby agree with the annually duly-elected representatives of the clubs of the National Basketball Association to meet with them during the annual meeting of said Board of Governors at a mutually-agreeable time for the discussion and action on matters of mutual benefit to the team owners and players.

At a meeting held at St. Louis on Thursday, April 18, 1957, a series of matters were discussed and the following action was taken by the Board of Governors with the approval of the team representatives:

1. On a probationary basis, the rule is established that a fine shall not be imposed on a player unless, at the time of the imposition, it is accompanied by a technical foul. [This meant the end of the hated "whispering fine."]

2. Each basketball player, while on the road, shall be paid seven dollars per diem expense money in addition to reasonable travel expenses.

3. The Board of Governors will increase the playoff pool for the season 1957-58 after a complete review of the season just concluded and past seasons.

4. Regular players will not be required to attend training camp earlier than four weeks prior to the starting date of the team of which the player is a member.

5. Exhibition games shall not be played on the three days prior to the opening of a team schedule nor on a day prior to a regularly scheduled game. Exhibition games during the regularly scheduled season shall not exceed three per team.

6. The proposed contract for each basketball player shall be forwarded to him by mail or delivered personally not later than September 1 of each year.

7. In the event of a dispute between a player and a club, the matter of dispute shall be referred to the N.B.A. President, and if the player does not approve the President's decision, the decision shall be appealed to a committee of three N.B.A. Governors, all of whom are to be chosen by the player. The decision of any two of the Governors shall be binding.

8. The matter of appearances on radio and/or television shall be considerately treated by the team owner and the player with due regard for the player.

9. In the event that a player's contract is transferred during the course of a season, the reasonable expenses of moving a player and his family from city to city shall be paid by the assignee club.

The within and foregoing represents the agreement of the Board of Governors of the National Basketball Association executed by the President of the Association hereunto duly authorized.

[Signed] Maurice Podoloff

Every bit of the smoldering resentment I'd ever felt against Podoloff evaporated when I saw his signature on that document. From that time on I was at peace with the world and the National Basketball Association.

I7 *Anxiety*

I HAVE OFTEN BEEN ASKED HOW I CAN STAND THE PRESSURES of my normal life both off and on the basketball court. The year 1957 was a pretty typical one. The Celtics were in action from January to mid-April, and I was on the exhibition tour from the day after the final playoffs to early May. I was home for two days and then went to Europe for five weeks. After a week at home, Missie went with me to Puerto Rico. The day after we got home we went to camp for the summer. When that was over, I made appearances in several places around the eastern part of the country until it was time for the new N.B.A. season to begin.

This was not unusual for me; I've always thrived on a fast pace. I must have millions of ergs of excess energy. It's hard for me to relax. Usually, I can get a tremendous lift from comparatively little sleep. Sometimes a nap in a cab on the way from some airport to a hotel will set me up for the next twenty-four hours.

I have to be moving all the time. If I'm not playing basketball, I've got to play something else. Tennis and handball have always been hobbies of mine, and I've recently become deeply interested in golf. I can't stand inactivity. It's worse for me than overactivity. As a matter of fact, I get nightmares when things are too quiet.

I'm a nightmare man from way back. Even when I was a kid on the East Side of New York, I used to walk and talk in my sleep. My mother found me one night sitting on a ledge and hanging on to the grillwork, three flights above East End Avenue. She hauled me in, and I woke up screaming in French.

In St. Albans, I once dreamed I was in a speeding car. The faster the car went, the more anxious I was to jump out of it. I was yelling in French when my mother woke me up, just in time to keep me from jumping twenty feet to the sidewalk.

For years I spoke French in my sleep. Since my marriage I've continued to *parler* in French except when Missie talks to me in English. Then I answer in English. I told her I had nightmares before we were married, and though she was prepared for the first one, she was considerably startled. She woke up to see me wandering around muttering to myself in French.

"Where are you going?" she asked me.

"Once around the bed," I answered in English.

So I walked once around the bed and then climbed back in. I didn't know a thing about it until Missie told me the next morning.

I never had nightmares during the basketball season. I guess I used up all the excess energy on the floor. I was usually so active in the off-season that it didn't happen very often. And until I got into camp work, I hadn't had a nightmare for a couple of years.

Even after camp started, I had only a few very harmless nightmares. Missie could always handle me. She would talk softly to me, and I'd often go back to bed without even waking up.

But during the summer of 1956, after a particularly active year, I nearly went berserk. I had gone from one extreme to the other. First of all, after the season ended, I traveled extensively, rushing to make planes and exhibition games and thriving on it. Then I suddenly found myself in a quiet, peaceful cottage in Pittsfield, New Hampshire, with my wife and two daughters. My life was busy but regular. I got up at the same time every morning, went through the same routine, ate at the same hours and went to bed early. It should have been a perfect rest period after tremendous activity.

But one night I had a bad dream. I started yelling in French, throwing punches and trying to run away. I found out later that I'd jumped out of bed, pushed Missie aside and paid no attention to her attempts to quiet me. Then I'd run out of the bedroom, punched open an oak door, dashed through the kitchen and the living room and punched my way through the screen door leading outside. And all the time I'd been yelling in French.

Once outside, I'd run squarely into my car, parked in the driveway, before turning and running down a hill toward camp. By this time Missie was following and screaming at me to wake up. I finally did when I crashed into a tree. By that time half the camp was awake wondering what all the fuss was about.

I had two skinned knees and a broken finger and was bleeding like a stuck pig. The camp doctor gave me shots for blood poisoning, and after a day or so, I was back in my normal routine. It took the finger a few weeks to heal, but except for my ego, I didn't ruffle much of anything. I was a little embarrassed because I'd disturbed so many people. And

I was afraid I might have hurt Missie since I'd tried to punch her when she caught up with me after I hit my car. Everything seemed to settle down, however, and I thought no more about it. It seemed to be just another nightmare, more violent than the usual but nothing to be alarmed about.

But almost exactly the same thing happened again in mid-August. I dreamed that I was trapped and held by a gang, and I had to punch my way out. As I dreamed I was being chased, I ran all the way to the nearest camp hut and crashed through a screen porch before someone woke me up. Although I didn't suffer any broken bones this time, I was bruised and hurt—and scared to death.

I'd never done this before, and now it had happened twice in a month.

"You've got to see a doctor," Missie said.

"I've seen one," I told her.

"I think you ought to go to a psychiatrist," she said. "You've never had nightmares this bad before. Why don't you go to Worcester tomorrow?"

So the next day I went to Worcester.

"You've got an anxiety complex," the doctor told me.

"An anxiety complex?" I said. "Why, I'm the calmest guy in the world! I never get excited!"

"That's what you think," he said, "You're burning up inside. You have to be moving all the time or you're in trouble. You're used to jumping around, and up there in camp you're staying in one place. You're living too sedentary a life."

"But I'm working there all the time," I said. "I'm running around with the kids and playing basketball with them and all that."

"And you're not under one bit of pressure," he pointed out. "Your life is geared to a fast-moving pace and you thrive on excitement."

"What should I do—get excited at camp?" I asked.

"No," he said. "I'll give you something to take every night. See how it works."

So I took pills for the rest of the summer, and it worked fine. I didn't have any more nightmares. Then when camp was over and I was back in my normally hectic routine, I didn't have to take the pills any more. Whenever I'm at camp now, I take a pill before going to bed, and I haven't had a nightmare since.

18 *The hungry game*

I'VE OFTEN THOUGHT ABOUT THIS NEED FOR EXCITEMENT AND pressure. Of course, it stems originally from my parents, particularly my mother, who has always had tremendous excess energy, but there is more to it than that. I grew up "hungry" in a sense—not that I ever actually starved. But money was always a problem, and because of this I worked hard and played hard. I play hard to this day, even though I'm no longer a so-called hungry athlete.

If you've had to fight for everything as a child, you'll fight after you're grown up. Johnny Bach, the Fordham basketball coach, deliberately combed the slum areas of New York for talent.

"I'd rather have a hungry little guy," he used to say, "than a well-fed big one. The ideal player is a hungry big guy. He's got the build and the will to win too. But if I'm going to get one or the other, I'll take the will to win."

I agree with him. The will to win can make up for a lack of many things, including build, which is so important in basketball. Sleater (Dugey) Martin of the St. Louis Hawks is two inches under six feet, but he's been an N.B.A. star for years. Whitey Skoog, formerly of Minneapolis, isn't a six-footer, but he was a star for a long time. Dick McGuire of the Knickerbockers is an even six feet, but he'll outplay guys six inches taller. Bobby Wanzer, for years a standout with the Royals and now their coach, stands only six feet.

None of those guys had it easy growing up; they were all hungry athletes. As a matter of fact, ninety-five per cent of all professional athletes started out that way. I've never heard of a rich kid becoming a star professional, although I suppose there must have been a few. But there weren't many.

Sometimes you hear a guy say, "Well, if we get the breaks, we might be all right." For my money, that's so much malarkey. You don't *get* breaks, you *make* them. Sure, you get lucky occasionally, but most of the time you hustle for the breaks because you want to win so badly.

Some guys don't even have much natural ability, but they fight hard enough to end up playing on even terms with their natural superiors. Al McGuire, Dick's brother, was a classic example of this. He played for the Knickerbockers four or five years with not much else except desire and the will to win to keep him going.

We had a guy like that—Bob Brannum. He was a big, awkward fellow who had to learn everything the hard way. He didn't look very pretty out on the basketball floor, but he got things done. And because he worked so hard they had to play him in spots. He gave everything he had every minute he was in there, but he would have killed himself if he had stayed in too long at a time.

Brannum was a farm boy who had worked hard all his life. By the time he came into the league, he had long since learned that he'd have to do things the hard way. His wonderful competitive spirit has served as an inspiration to me ever since I first met him. I'm glad I've got that spirit. I wouldn't swap it for anything.

The St. Louis Hawks nearly beat us in the finals of the N.B.A. playoffs in the spring of 1957 because every one of them had that terrific urge to win. I was hoping that they would lose in the Western Division finals to Minneapolis because even though the Lakers had a better ball club than St. Louis, they didn't have the Hawks' fight and will to win. And when St. Louis won that series, I knew we were in for trouble. They hustled and fought and played over their heads against us, and it wasn't until the second overtime of the final game that we beat them. Man for man, we were a better ball club and so was Minneapolis.

Everyone notices that I'm a poker-faced character, but I don't feel poker-faced. I might have told that Worcester doctor that I never get excited, but I didn't mean it. From the minute I get up, I'm all goose-pimples on the day of a big game. I don't sleep well, I eat poorly and my stomach leaps. I do whatever I can to get my mind off the game: go to the movies, play cards, carry on business affairs—anything at all—and the people with me swear I don't bat an eye.

"That Cousy," I heard a friend tell a guy during the playoffs in 1957, "he's got no nerves. On the day of a game in St. Louis, he worked all afternoon with one of his business associates, then played a hell of a game that night."

I've got news for you. "That Cousy" was scared to death all day.

But once the whistle blows and the game starts, I'm fine. It's as if someone had opened up the valves and let out all the steam. My head clears, my nerves stop jumping and my stomach behaves. And no matter how fast I'm traveling on the floor or how hard I'm playing, I'm able to think clearly so that I can take advantage of any opening.

No matter how tough the pressure or how hard I work, I'm always more tired after a losing game than a victory. I can go at top speed for all but a few minutes of a winning game, and I feel fresh when it's over. But if I play only half the time in a losing cause, I'm dished at the end. Of course, this is purely psychological. Hours later, after a victory, I get a physical letdown that leaves me weak as a rag.

I'm a lousy loser. I don't hold with these Pollyanna theories about the game being the thing. That may be the right and proper thing to do, but it doesn't go with me. When I lose, I don't feel like congratulating the winner and shaking his hand. I want to go into a corner and mope. I do all my hand-shaking and congratulating later, after the heat of the game has dissipated.

But while the game is on—and immediately before and after it—I'm a hard guy to get along with. I hate everybody except my teammates. When friends wave to me from the stands, I don't pay any attention to them. I've got my mind on one thing: to beat the daylights out of the other team; and I can't think of anything else once I get out on the floor.

I'll sign autographs until the cows come home if I have time after I'm showered and dressed, but I'm a dead-pan stinker as I return to the locker room directly after a game. I can't help it. That's the way I'm built.

Ever since I was president of what they called General Organization at Andrew Jackson High School in St. Albans, I've had to speak in public. Later, during my years at Holy Cross, I had to do it more often, and now it's part of my regular routine.

Originally, I was terrified at the thought of getting up on my feet in front of a crowd of people. I used to stutter and stammer around and say in a practically inaudible voice, "We'll—uh—do our best. Thank you." Then I'd sit down amid crash-

ing applause from an audience made up of kids who loved me
because I was the basketball co-captain. But in college I realized that I couldn't get away with this sort of thing forever. I
read books about public speaking and practiced in front of
a mirror. I also did everything I could to improve my vocabu-
lary.

I never really got used to after-dinner speaking. Even today I get a slight case of butterflies just before I get on my
feet, but just as in a basketball game, it all goes away the minute I start talking.

I've always tried to set goals for myself. When we first
started playing basketball around St. Albans, Angus Kennedy,
my pal and neighbor, developed a little faster than I did. My
first goal was to catch up with him.

After I started in high school, I had a new goal. Frank
Higgins, who lived in St. Albans, was a Boston College bas-
ketball star, and I wanted to be as good as he was. And once
I got to Holy Cross, my goal was to make All-America.

I was thrilled by the publicity I got right from the beginning, although I was always careful not to show it. I kept a
scrapbook and read everything they wrote about me while
I was in college. I don't keep the scrapbook any more (Missie
and my mother do that), but I still read about myself, and I
still get a kick out of it.

I never kidded myself about publicity or sports fame. I
have a loathing for people who are affected by the publicity
they get. I can't stand affectation or lack of sincerity. I have
no use for back-slappers and front-runners. When people tell
me how good they think I am, I thank them and hope they
mean it. But I've always tried not to let it go to my head.

I've known guys with big heads; unfortunately the woods
are full of them. There might be an excuse for it at college
age. A college kid doesn't have enough resistance to adula-

tion in big doses. But how a grown man can allow his head to be turned by this sort of thing is beyond me.

My religion has helped me keep my feet on the ground. I know I should be a better Catholic. I get to Communion as often as I can, and I very rarely miss church. I get more out of my Catholicism than I put in. They say religion is good for the very young and the very old. I am neither, but it gives me an outlet for problems. When I have problems, I go to church for guidance. I don't solve my problems that way, but I get peace of mind when I need it.

One of the nicest things that ever happened to me was when my parish priest in Worcester told me after Mass one Sunday, "Bob, every time you walk down the aisle where the children can see you, it's better than my preaching a sermon on Communion."

It made me feel good, and it made me realize that I have a responsibility to my neighbors.

When you grow up poor, you realize that all people are basically the same. Poverty is a great leveler. A poor Catholic is closer to a poor Jew than to a rich Catholic. A poor Protestant is closer to a poor Catholic than to a rich Protestant. It works the other way too. A rich Catholic is closer to a rich Protestant than to a poor Catholic.

I once saw a guy scrawl on a fence in Worcester, "Down with the Jews!"

"What's the matter with the Jews?" I asked him.

"I don't like them," he said.

"Why?" I said.

He hesitated. Finally he said, "Well, my mother and father told me they were no good."

This is the kind of screwy logic that infuriates me. I reserve the right to dislike whoever I want, but I have to have a better reason than that for disliking him.

I've got just as little patience with the drawing of the color line. Negro players are vital members of teams in all sports, and basketball is no exception. As it happened, I had never had a colored teammate until I joined the Celtics. Chuck Cooper also joined us that year. Cooper, who came from Pittsburgh, was and still is one of my closest friends. We often roomed together on the road when he was with the Celtics. During the autumn when Missie and the kids were living in Walter Brown's home on Cape Cod, Cooper and I shared an apartment in Boston.

The Celtics once played an exhibition game in Raleigh, North Carolina. Cooper, who had never been south of the Mason-Dixon Line, was very sensitive about his situation because he knew he would be faced with problems of prejudice. He couldn't stay in the hotel with us, he couldn't eat with us, and he couldn't even go to the movies with us.

We were supposed to play that night, then fly to New York in the morning. But after the game I could see that Cooper was very blue. I was embarrassed for him, and since he couldn't stay in the hotel, I wondered what his plans were. I asked Red Auerbach.

"He's taking a late sleeper out," said Red.

"Mind if I go with him?" I asked.

"Go ahead."

Chuck and I walked around town to kill time; the train came through around three in the morning. But while there was still time, we wanted to get a couple of cans of beer in a package store near the railroad station. There were two entrances, one labeled "White," the other "Colored."

Neither of us said anything. We just walked away.

Later we went back to the station, and there we saw the signs again—"White" with an arrow pointing to one waiting room and "Colored" with an arrow pointing to the other.

All night we'd studiously avoided the subject. I felt as though I were at a wake. Finally I spoke up.

"The colored aren't the only ones who are persecuted," I said. "Hitler persecuted the Jews and so did a lot of others. And I was just reading in the papers where they threw bombs at Catholic churches somewhere in Louisiana not long ago."

Chuck looked at me a minute. Then he said quietly, "That's all right, but you can't always tell a Jew or a Catholic by looking at him."

I changed the subject quickly. And when the train arrived I couldn't get on it fast enough to shake the dust of Raleigh from my feet.

19 *High jinks*

THE WORLD IS FULL OF UNUSUAL CHARACTERS, AND SOME of them are involved in professional basketball. One of the funniest guys I ever knew was a long, skinny Celtics' teammate of mine named Bones McKinney, who looked so much like Ichabod Crane he should have been a schoolteacher. As a matter of fact, he was a part-time preacher when he played pro basketball and is now a minister somewhere down south.

Bones was with the Celtics in the days when they were struggling to stay in existence, let alone win anything. But no matter how badly things were going, he always had a grin on his homely face, and he was always good for a laugh. A great showman, he once brought a Boston Garden house down when he reached a ball that was going out of bounds, slipped and landed squarely in the lap of a lady in the front row. He smirked, patted her on the head and posed for a minute while the lady joined the crowd in convulsed laughter. Bones should have been with the Harlem Globetrotters. He knew many of their tricks. I've seen him shoot fouls with his back to the hoop, and he rarely missed.

He was the only professional basketball player I ever knew who wouldn't fly in a plane. He went everywhere by train, even though it meant being late to a ball game at times or even missing one altogether.

"If the Good Lord had intended for me to fly," he used to say, "He'd have provided me with wings. I don't mind going when my own time comes, but I'm darned if I intend to go along with some strange pilot when *his* time comes."

I wasn't so many years away from understanding how he felt. Only three years before, I'd flown for the first time, and it was a harrowing experience that kept me on the ground for two years.

It happened when Holy Cross went down to the Sugar Bowl tournament. The air was so rough that we seemed to bounce all over the sky. Not knowing any better, I figured all airplane trips were like that. I didn't even have the brains to get sick. But as we approached St. Louis, one of our stops en route, I looked down and saw fire engines and ambulances on the field.

"What the devil are those for?" I asked my seat-mate. He was too green around the gills to answer. I rang for the stewardess, but she didn't show up. So I unbuckled my seat belt and stood up to see if I could find her. She was in back of the plane, as sick as everyone else. That's when I got scared. If the stewardess could get sick and crash crews were waiting for us to land, I figured this was no racket for me.

We got down safely, but after we landed, I went over to Doggie Julian and said, "You'll never get Mrs. Cousy's boy into an airplane again."

We went the rest of the way by train.

Later I learned the advantages of flying, and I go everywhere by plane today. But not Bones McKinney. He spent more time on trains than anyone I ever knew. The Celtics never stayed in one place longer than it took to play a game and maybe get a night's sleep. But Bones had to do all his sleeping on the rails.

He lived a lonesome life. Once he barged into the locker room and pleaded, "Speak to me, someone! I've been all by myself on trains for two days! I feel like a hermit!"

Bones remained true to terra firma throughout his basketball career in spite of what happened to him in 1952. That year the team flew about 30,000 miles without incident. Bones didn't fly a mile, but he was in three minor train wrecks and a taxicab crash.

Togo Palazzi, who came out of Holy Cross and was with the Celtics for a couple of years before he was traded to Syracuse, was another guy who was usually good for a laugh. Togo was a man of idiosyncrasies. He had so many superstitions he couldn't keep track of them all.

In St. Louis he once sat next to the cab driver on the way from the hotel to the airport. Halfway out, someone called his attention to a sign on the dashboard which read: "This is the suicide seat. Please do not sit here unless absolutely necessary." I don't believe Togo has sat next to a cab driver since, at least not in St. Louis.

Ever since college Togo has had a complex about being the last man out of the locker room before a game. When we found out about it, we used to stall until the very last minute, trying to get Togo to go out ahead of us. He would hide in the shower or behind a trunk until everyone had gone, then he'd walk out.

One night, just before the opening whistle of a game in Fort Wayne, we were huddled together, as usual, waiting for Red's last-minute instructions. He started to say something, then straightened up and asked, "Where's Togo?"

Everyone looked at everyone else. Suddenly Bill Sharman started laughing.

"I'll bet he's still in the locker room," he said. "I was trying to make him go out ahead of me, and he disappeared."

Auerbach sent someone in after him. Sure enough, there was Togo pounding on the door and screaming his head off. He'd been locked in for twenty minutes!

○

When I first joined the Celtics, we trained at Ellsworth, Maine, a lovely little town where they treated us like kissing cousins. Among other things, they delivered Boston daily newspapers every morning to each guy on the squad. These papers arrived at about five in the morning.

Bill Mokray of the Boston Garden publicity staff went up there with us at that time. Mokray, one of the best-informed basketball men I ever knew, was conscientious to the point of fussiness. He conceived the idea of getting up early, collecting the papers from in front of our rooms and sending clippings about the Celtics to the people on his mailing list.

It took us a few days to discover what was happening to our papers. When we found out, we checked to see what time Mokray got up. I think it was about seven in the morning, which, of course, was much too early for us. But one day I got up at 6:30. I collected all the papers, carefully clipped out the sports pages from each and left a note that read, "The Phantom was here." Then I put the papers back where I found them and went back to bed.

Mokray was fit to be tied. When we all got up later, he growled, "Who's the wise guy?"

The next morning 6:30 was too late. When I got up, the

papers were gone. So the morning after, I was up at 6:00. The papers were intact, and I clipped them again. And later Mokray was walking around talking to himself.

The morning after, 6:00 wasn't early enough. Mokray had beat me to it. The situation was getting ridiculous so I enlisted Bill Sharman's aid. He was up at 5:30, in time to clip the papers the next morning. He got somebody else for the day after. Pretty soon guys were getting up before the papers came. By that time we were sick of the game and so was Mokray.

○

Red Auerbach is also a very fussy man, particularly about his clothes. Sometimes Red will show up in such sartorial splendor he nearly blinds us.

He came around in Maine one time wearing a gorgeous red fedora with a snappy brim, which he carefully set at the exact angle he wanted before going out every day. He'd brush it daily, sometimes spending as much as half an hour working on it. Then he'd stand in front of a mirror for five or ten minutes fixing it just the way he wanted it.

He guarded that fedora like the crown jewels. Even when he took a shower, he placed it on a chair where he could look at it from time to time to make sure it was all right.

One day he was whistling in his shower when suddenly all hell broke loose. He dashed out, naked and dripping and screaming, "Where's my hat? Who's the dirty so-and-so who took my hat?"

"Now, Red, don't get excited," I said. "I know exactly where your hat is."

"Cousy," he howled, "if you did anything to that hat, so help me, I'll murder you!"

"I didn't do a thing to it, old boy," I said.

"Well, where is it?"

"Right there," I said calmly and pointed to an adjoining shower where Ed Macauley was happily scrubbing himself while the water cascaded down. He was wearing Red's precious hat.

Red made a dive for Macauley. Ed pulled the hat off and threw the dripping mess to me. I had a scissiors, and before Red could reach me, I was busy cutting the hat into small pieces.

We thought poor Red would explode. He called Macauley and me names that would curl your hair. And when he stomped out of there, he was still bleating like a wounded elephant.

He didn't quiet down until he'd reached his car and found a brand new red fedora, which the whole club had chipped in to buy for him. After that the hat stayed in his car, which Red was always careful to lock.

○

One of the funniest guys we ever had on the Celtics was Gene Conley, the Milwaukee Braves pitcher who could have been a great basketball player if the Braves had let him continue with us. Six feet, eight inches tall, he had a grin like Bones McKinney and a wonderful droll sense of humor.

He spent the 1952 season with the old Milwaukee Brewers since the Braves were still in Boston at the time. He lived in Richland, Washington, and in his college days he had been both a basketball and baseball star at Washington State.

Richland is two thousand miles west of Milwaukee. Boston is a thousand miles east. One day, shortly after the baseball sea-

son ended, Conley showed up in Boston. His wife and youngster were with him, and his car was loaded. He had come to
sign a basketball contract with the Celtics.

Newspapermen covering the Garden couldn't miss the guy;
so a press conference was called. The first question a writer
asked Conley was, "What are you doing here?"

"Well, I'll tell you," he said. "I was on my way home to
Richland from Milwaukee, and I just dropped by to say hello."

We used to barnstorm around northern New England on
the way back to Boston from Ellsworth in those days. Gene
always posed as Macauley, and it drove Ed crazy. We'd go
to a club dinner in some small town in the sticks, and Conley
would take over as Macauley. One night after he had signed
Macauley's autograph for half an hour, somebody asked him
about St. Louis University, Macauley's alma mater.

"A joint," Gene replied. "The only reason I went there
was because I couldn't get in anywhere else."

"That's a fine way to talk about your own school," the man
said. "I'll bet they gave you a scholarship to go there too."

"A scholarship?" said Conley. "They not only gave me a
scholarship, but I got four hundred bucks a month spending
money and a new car every year."

Macauley, who was as convulsed as the rest of us, was just
about to speak up when a baseball fan asked where Conley
was.

"He must have sneaked out," Gene said. "I think he's
ashamed of himself."

"Why?"

"For taking money to play baseball. He's one of the world's
lousiest pitchers."

That broke us up.

20 *Flying high*

I NORMALLY TRAVEL SOMEWHERE BETWEEN THIRTY-FIVE and fifty thousand miles a year, and I must have hit the seventy-five thousand mark in 1957. In the natural course of events we go about twenty-five thousand miles during the basketball season. I went ten thousand more on the barnstorming trip I took in 1957 and fifteen to twenty thousand more on the trip to Europe that followed. Puerto Rico, including travel on the island, made another five thousand, and I don't know how many miles more I tacked up in side trips around the East.

Red Auerbach and I went to Europe on a State Department good will tour in May of 1957 to introduce and demonstrate basketball techniques in various countries abroad. Red did the lecturing, and I did the demonstrating. People in most of the places we hit had never seen the game played. Red had to start from scratch, and because English is the only tongue he knows, he operated under a handicap.

Actually my French got us by in most of the countries we visited, and when we were with French-speaking people, I did the translating. However, we usually needed an interpreter. French took care of our daily needs, but we often worked before large groups of people who knew no French. This resulted in some interesting situations. Naturally, Red had to talk at some length in order to explain his points, particularly when he was addressing people who had never heard of the game. I had a tough time keeping a straight face a couple of times.

Once in Turkey, Red yakked for ten or fifteen minutes. When he got through, the interpreter said about three words. Red threw up his hands and bleated, "Jeepers, is that all I said!"

Wherever we went, people seemed interested in basketball. In Porta, Portugal, four hundred people listened to us while we talked and worked for two hours in a driving rainstorm. We spent five days in Portugal, then went to Belgium, Denmark, Austria, Turkey and Iran. We planned to spend some time in Rome and Nice, but I got sick in the Near East, and we had to cut the trip short. We did go to Rome for a couple of days, but I staggered around in a fog.

I would have come straight home from Iran except that I wanted to meet my long-lost half-sister, Blanche Pettuy. She is sixteen years older than I and has a married daughter. She lives in Nice, and when I took sick, she flew to Rome to meet me. Blanche is my father's daughter by a previous marriage. When my parents came to the States, she remained in France with the understanding that she would follow them over here. But she got married and never did make the trip.

Somehow or other, my family lost contact with her for nearly thirty years. Then my father got a letter from her. I was all excited since I had been brought up an only child and had always missed not having a brother or sister. I picked up the correspondence, and Blanche and I had been writing each other regularly ever since.

I learned from her where some of my own athletic ability came from. Some years back France had a national women's championship basketball team, and she played on it. She is also an enthusiastic mountain climber, skier and tennis player. I was sorry I was so sick when I finally met her that I couldn't spend as much time with her as I'd wanted. Some day I hope to bring her here since she's dead set on coming to the United States.

I first got sick on a plane in Iran flying from Ishfahan to Abadan. I can look back and laugh about it now, but I was the most miserable basketball player in the world when the thing first hit me. Red, who practically saved my life, told me later he thought I was going to die, which at the time would have suited me fine.

My trouble was a fairly common ailment among tourists. In the Near East it's called Teheran Tummy. It has other names in other parts of the world, but it all adds up to the same thing: an acute intestinal ailment which, they tell me, can actually kill you.

When I first began to feel bad, I thought it was just another stomach ache. On the plane I told Red I felt lousy, and he agreed with me when I suggested I was suffering from something I'd eaten plus the intense heat and the movement of the plane.

I got sicker and sicker. After we landed in Abadan and I kept feeling worse, Red began to get worried. I have only a vague recollection of getting off the plane. We arrived about 10:30 in the morning and were met by a welcoming committee, including some school kids with flowers, a guy from the U.S.I.S. and another man representing an oil company.

I couldn't get down the steps of the plane without leaning heavily on Red, and when one of the children threw a wreath of flowers around my neck, I nearly collapsed from its weight.

The heat was unbearable. I found out later that it was one hundred and twenty degrees in the shade, a bracing day for Abadan. I guess that was about twenty degrees cooler than normal there.

We were supposed to give a basketball clinic at 6:30 that night. The guy from the U.S.I.S. looked at me and said, "Too much airplane?"

"Too much something he ate," Red said. "Got a doctor in this place?"

"I don't need a doctor," I mumbled weakly. "Just let me get a few hours' sleep in the hotel, and I'll be all right."

The U.S.I.S. guy seemed sort of doubtful, but he said, "That might do it. The clinic isn't until 6:30."

"What happened?" asked the guy from the oil company.

"I don't know," I murmured.

"Cramps?" he asked. "Stomach ache?"

I nodded.

"Chills and fever?"

I nodded again.

"Brother," he said, "you've had it. You won't know your name by 6:30 tonight."

He was right. I don't remember much else. I know a doctor came around, put his hand on my head and said, "You've got a fever of about 105."

"How do you know?" asked Red.

"I can tell," he said.

"Why don't you take his temperature with a thermometer?" Red asked.

"We don't have any thermometers in Abadan. This man will lose twenty pounds."

Then he walked away.

"Please, Red," I whispered. "Get me somewhere where they have thermometers."

The next thing I remember was somebody putting a thermometer in my mouth.

"Where are we?" I asked.

"Teheran," Red said.

"I knew it wasn't Abadan," I muttered.

The doctor in Abadan was right. I did lose twenty pounds in about three days. Red canceled the rest of the trip and wired my sister to meet me in Rome. We got home a week ahead of schedule. And I didn't feel myself again until I got up to camp.

⊙

Ever since I graduated from Holy Cross in 1950, I've wanted to be in camp work. I enjoy kids, and I wanted to plan a long-range career which would keep me around them.

My friend Jimmy O'Connell from Holy Cross, through whom I met Joe Sharry, and I tried unsuccessfully to locate a camp site a few years after I got out of college. Then I met J. A. Geib of New York and his two sons, Bob and Fred. They were the owners of Camp Graylag in Pittsfield, New Hampshire. They asked me if I'd be interested in going in with them. I would be sort of a general director, supervising the athletic program and helping to bring in campers.

This was exactly the sort of setup I was looking for. The Geibs had the camp and the capital, and I had the opportunity to get around the country, attract boys to the camp and run a sports program. We've had a very happy relationship ever since, and we've brought in boys from nearly every state in the Union.

Naturally my top thrills have come on the basketball court, but I've gotten terrific charges out of four off-court events

which stemmed directly from basketball. One was the news
that the N.B.A. had agreed to recognize the Basketball Players'
Association. Another was being invited to the White House for
a Presidential luncheon along with star athletes of other sports.
A third was a testimonial banquet given in my honor in
Worcester in 1954. My parents say that this was *their* greatest
thrill, and I guess it must have been since they shared the lime-
light with me. In 1956 I also got a kick out of being the only
athlete named as one of Greater Boston's ten outstanding
young men by the Junior Chamber of Commerce.

The Presidential invitation was a happy surprise which
caused a near-panic in the Cousy household. Missie is a great
letter-writer, a viewer-with-alarm who likes to try to carry the
weight of the world on her shoulders. She was forever writing
to Congressman Harold Donohue of Worcester about some civic
wrong which should be righted or some international incident
which should be given immediate attention. And she didn't stop
with Congressman Donohue.

In 1955 Missie was very much upset about the Argentina
situation. Peron had been excommunicated, and I guess there
was some question in Missie's mind as to how the United States
stood on the situation. So she sat right down and wrote a letter
to Harold Stassen, pointing out certain things that she felt he
should know.

Much to Missie's amazement, she received a reply from Stassen. In the same mail, she got a letter from Congressman Donohue about something else. And in the same mail a letter came
for me. She glanced at it, noted that the return address was the
White House and put it in my pile of mail so that I could open
it when I got home.

We have a friend in Worcester who runs a restaurant called
the White House. Missie hadn't even looked at the postmark;
she simply took if for granted that this letter was from him.

I got home the next day, and Missie said, "You know who I got a letter from?"

"Congressman Donohue!" I said brightly.

"Yes, and someone else."

"Who?" I asked.

"Harold Stassen."

"Well, I'll be jiggered," I said.

Then I sat down to open my own mail.

When I reached the letter from the White House, my first reaction was similar to Missie's; I thought it was from our friend in Worcester. But when I saw the Washington postmark, I realized how wrong we both were.

I tore open the letter and looked at the signature of Dwight D. Eisenhower.

"Hey, Missie!" I yelled. "Come here—quick!"

"What's the matter?" she asked.

"You get letters from Congressmen?" I said. "You get letters from Harold Stassen? Look who I got a letter from!"

I don't think Missie has ever quite forgiven me.

The Presidential letter was an invitation to a sports luncheon at the White House which was supposed to attract national attention to the problem of physical inactivity among our youth. A survey had revealed that fifty-six per cent of American boys couldn't pass basic physical exams while in Europe only eight per cent failed.

I got a big kick out of the whole affair, particularly the chance to shake hands with the President and to sit down and talk with some of the great athletes in American sports. I was the only professional basketball player there. College basketball was represented by Bill Russell, then at San Francisco University, who later became a Celtics teammate of mine.

CHAPTER	21	*My All-America*
		team

RUSSELL MAY SOME DAY BE THE GREATEST BASKETBALL center of all time, but based on the record, George Mikan would have to be the center on my All-America team. Mikan, who stood 6′ 10″ and weighed 220 pounds, had the best height and weight combination I ever saw. I'll take twenty pounds in weight over two inches in height at that level because a center must be strong as well as tall.

Despite his bulk, Mikan was a graceful athlete, and he had that terrific will to win. He was a real fighter all the way and never let up when he was out on the court. He was a good shooter, a good rebound man and more than adequate defensively. When he was playing, the guy was in a class by himself.

For forwards, I'll take Bob Pettit of the St. Louis Hawks and Dolph Schayes of the Syracuse Nats. Pettit, 6′ 9″ and 210 pounds, also has a great height-weight combination. He moves around like a man 6′ 4″, and he's very fast and very tricky. He's a good shot, and I think the hardest man to defend I ever saw. And he is quite capable of stealing the ball from time to time. He almost killed us in the 1957 playoffs by keeping the Hawks alive up to the last minute.

At 6′ 8″, 220 pounds, Schayes is another ideally built player. It's nearly as hard to do a good defensive job on him as on Pettit. He drives well, is a great rebound man and can shoot with either hand. In my opinion, he's also the best outside shooter of the big men.

For guards I'll take Bill Sharman of the Celtics and Sleater Martin of the Hawks. Sharman is the greatest shooter the game has ever known. There's been no one in the history of basketball who could hit as consistently from the foul line. He also has the best one-handed set shot and the best jump shot I've ever seen. He's absolutely tremendous defensively and can rag and worry opponents to death. Bill's a good, sound, all-around player. In fact, there's no one in the league so outstanding in so many different ways.

Martin, the smallest guy on my All-America team, is another great defensive player. In my seven years in the league, he's given me more trouble than anyone else. He's an amazingly accurate shooter who has all the shots. He also has a tremendous desire to win which has helped him overcome his height handicap.

Paul Walther of Philadelphia and Gene Shue of Fort Wayne (now Detroit) were also great defensively. I've had nearly as much trouble with those guys—though not over as long a period of years—as I've had with Martin.

I would say that as new as he is in the league, Bill Russell is the best rebounder I ever saw. He is big—6′ 10″—very fast and a cat when it comes to grabbing the ball. In the short time he was with the Celtics in 1957 he set several records for rebounds, and he'll get better before he gets worse.

When it comes to faking from side to side, I'll take Sharman. Carl Braun of the New York Knickerbockers has the best up-and-down fake I've ever seen, and he and Schayes have the best two-handed set shots. When it comes to layups, give me George Dempsey of Philadelphia. And for jump-shooting by a big man, I'll take Pettit and Paul Arizin of Philadelphia.

The most amazing shot I ever heard of—I didn't see it because I was waiting for the ball to reach me—was Bill Sharman's basket from seventy feet out in the 1957 East-West All-Star game in Boston. I was down near the West basket and in the clear. Sharman had the ball near our basket at the other end of the court. He let go with what was meant to be a pass, but the ball got away from him. Instead of heading toward me, it went right through the hoop for the longest shot in the history of the pro game.

Everyone in the Boston Garden, which had a sellout crowd, was so stunned that for a minute there wasn't a sound. Then the whole place exploded. While Bill stood with his hands on his hips, as stunned as everyone else, the crowd roared. Guys on both the East and West teams walked over to shake his hand.

22 | *The big one*

I'VE HAD SOME GREAT THRILLS FROM BASKETBALL, BUT I guess I got my biggest kick on the afternoon of March 21, 1953, when we beat Syracuse 111 to 105 in a playoff game that went into four overtime periods. I scored 50 points that day, and it was a particularly sweet win for us because it got us by the first round of the Eastern Division finals.

It was a wild, woolly, almost unbelievable ball game, so close only three points separated the two teams at the end of each period. The Nats led 22-21 at the end of the first period and 42-40 at the close of the second. But we scored 22 to their 17 in the third to take over a 62-59 lead and lose it again when the Nats got 18 to our 15 in the fourth. That made it 77-77 at the end of the regulation four periods. Each club scored nine points in the first overtime, four in the second and nine in the third. Going into the fourth overtime, the score was 99-99. It was then that we broke the game wide open with 12 points to Syracuse's six, and that gave us our six-point margin of victory.

The sellout crowd was hysterical from the close of the

fourth period of regulation time to the end of the game. I found out later that Walter Brown couldn't look at the game after the third overtime period. He kept getting up from his seat, peeking every so often to get the score. And halfway through the fourth period the tension got so bad for Howie McHugh that he fainted dead away. It was all over and we had won before he was revived.

Meanwhile, out on the floor players on both teams were feeling the pressure too. In those days the league did not have the twenty-four-second rule, which says that no team can hold the ball more than twenty-four seconds without taking a shot. You could freeze the ball if you got possession, and we were freezing all day, which was why the score wasn't higher and each team got only four points in the second overtime. Occasional fights broke out, a couple of guys were thrown out, and everyone was jittery.

What made it such an outstanding game in my memory wasn't so much my point total but the fact that I hit with several clutch baskets. We were behind by a point in regulation time when I had to take a foul shot in the last seconds. When I sank it, the score went to 77-77 and the game into overtime.

In the first overtime period we were two behind when I scored in the last second. Of the nine points we had in that session I scored six. Both teams coasted in the second overtime, but fortunately I got hot again in the third. I scored eight of the Celtics' nine points that period. In the last second, I hit with a one-hander from center court to throw us into that tie. It was a desperation shot. We were two points behind, and it was our only chance to stay in the ball game. There wasn't time to pass to anyone. We broke open the game in the fourth overtime, and I had nine of our twelve points.

For scoring totals, this was the greatest game I ever played as a pro. I scored 30 foul shots in 32 tries, including 18 in a row. And in the last two overtimes I had to be careful because I had five personal fouls; six would have put me out of the game. It may sound like bragging, but that was one game I was proud of.

One other game that stands out in my mind is the East-West All-Star contest in Madison Square Garden in 1954. It was an 84-all tie at the end of regulation time. At that point the writers named Minneapolis' Jim Pollard, the game's high scorer, as the outstanding star. But we scored 14 points in the overtime for a 98-93 victory, and I had 10 of them. The writers polled themselves again and gave me the outstanding player award. They gave it to me again in the Boston game in 1957, but any one of half a dozen other guys could have got it then.

In spite of the fact that I was named to the N.B.A. All-Star team every year from 1951 on, I was never satisfied because the Celtics seemed to be able to do everything but win the championship. We finished second four times and third twice. We never got beyond the Eastern Division finals in playoffs and only got that far three times. It was not only very frustrating to us but to Boston's basketball fans and sports writers as well.

Red took the brunt of the blame for our failure to get to the top, but it wasn't his fault. As a matter of fact, Red transformed the Celtics from perennial losers to perennial threats. A look at the Celtics' records before he got there will prove that. They were last in 1947, their first year in the league, next to last the next two seasons and last again in 1950. Auerbach was hired immediately following that season, and we finished second in 1951. That was our first year in the playoffs, and we've never been out of them since.

Boston wanted a winner so badly that its critics forgot

Red's accomplishments and considered only what they called his failures. I'll admit that on paper it *was* frustrating, but we never had a thoroughly sound ball club until 1957, when we finally won everything.

In the first three years that I was with the club—and my time coincided with Red's—it began to look as though the New York Knickerbockers had a perpetual Indian sign on us. They beat us in the first round of the playoffs in 1951 and 1952, and then after our great game against Syracuse landed us in the Eastern finals in 1953, they beat us again.

For the next three years Syracuse was the cause of all our troubles. The Nats whipped us in 1954 after we survived a round robin series. The next year we got by the Knicks and lost to Syracuse again in the Eastern finals. And in 1956 the Nats eliminated us in the first round.

At the start of the 1956-57 season, we didn't look very much better on paper than we had in previous seasons; in fact, some observers thought we looked worse because we no longer had Ed Macauley. When we started out, we had only six men from the team which had finished second the year before. They were Bill Sharman, Jim Loscutoff, Arnie Risen, Jack Nichols, Dick Hemric and myself. Lou Tsioropoulos, who later became our eleventh man, was around, and there were two newcomers, the veteran Andy Phillip and Tom Heinsohn, the rookie fresh out of Holy Cross. Togo Palazzi, who was later traded to Syracuse, was also with us at the start of the season.

The club clicked from the start, and for my money, the man primarily responsible was Heinsohn. This twenty-three-year-old kid, youngest man on the squad, has the perfect build for a basketball player. He stands 6′ 7″ and weighs 220 pounds. He's fast, sure, and one of the greatest natural athletes I've ever seen. Beyond that, he has that wonderful will to win, so important if you ever hope to win anything.

Heinsohn simply refuses to admit he's licked. No matter what the odds against him are, he is fighting every minute. Not a second of his time on the floor is wasted. He's going at top speed from gun to gun and from whistle to whistle. He's got the stamina and the youth to keep going, and his drive keeps him on the ball all the time.

Tommy is a Brannum with natural ability. Where Brannum had to fight his way to the top by learning everything step by step, Heinsohn got there on ability and stayed there with the same kind of fight. He gave the Celtics something they had never had before: a great rebound man who could cope with the strongest men in the league. When we saw him in practice before the season began, we knew he'd make it, but I don't think any of us realized just how much he would mean to the team. He inspired us all with his drive, and we threatened to make a walkaway of the league race in the first six weeks.

Another guy who gave us something we hadn't had before was Jungle Jim Loscutoff. This was Loscutoff's second year in the league, but he was still feeling his way after his rookie season. Unlike Heinsohn, he needed that year of experience before he blossomed into a top star. At 6′ 5″ and 225 pounds, he has the kind of strength we needed. Like Heinsohn, he's got great natural ability and a tremendous desire to win, and like Heinsohn, he's rugged enough to fight the strongest men in the league on even terms. He also turned out to be a rebound artist, always in the thick of the fight to get the ball off the backboard.

What Celtics' critics never seemed to realize in previous years was that we never had really top-flight rebound men.

Ed Macauley was one of the greatest shots and finest centers in the business, but he was too frail to be a great rebound man. Our top guy in that department had been Jack Nichols, but he was a Tufts College dental student and could only play part-time. We needed a combination of strength and ability, and we had no one who answered both qualifications until Heinsohn and Loscutoff came along.

Those two would have made champions of the Celtics if the season had been cut in half. We already had Nichols and Risen for duty up front and Sharman and me in the back court. Before the season began we got Andy Phillip from Fort Wayne, and he did a great job of spelling Bill and me when we needed rest.

This was the backbone of our starting team for 1956-57, and we got rolling so quickly it looked as if no one was going to stop us. At one point we were five games in front of the field, and many experts were conceding the title to us before Christmas.

But we had little protection in case of injury, and we would have run into plenty of grief if we had had to depend entirely on this squad. Furthermore, we just couldn't keep up the pace. Sooner or later the race figured to even off. There was too much class in the rest of the league.

We were four games in front in December, but we all knew we had to have help. It came from two sources in almost the same week. Walter Brown signed Bill Russell to a Celtics contract, and within a matter of days after that, Frank Ramsey, a stickout with us two years before, came out of the army. The two couldn't have arrived at a more strategic time.

Risen had broken his arm and was out for the better part of the season. I wasn't up to par physically because I'd pulled a muscle. Loscutoff was out for a short time right after Russell and Ramsey reported. No other two players could have filled the gap as they did.

Russell turned out to be the hottest rebound man in basketball. When he, Heinsohn and Loscutoff were in action at one time, it took a miracle man to get the ball away from them off the backboard. Ramsey had always been a great back-court man. He and Phillip gave us terrific strength there whenever Sharman and I were on the sidelines together.

We sagged some because of our various injuries, but we pulled away again in early March and won the title going away. This gave us a much-needed and very welcome rest. It was the first time we had ever finished first. The division winner in the N.B.A. waits for the second and third teams to play their series, which determines the opponent of the first team for the division title.

Syracuse got by the Eastern semi-finals and then played us in the Eastern finals. This time we took no chance of losing the greatest opportunity we'd ever had. In the best three-for-five series we murdered the Nats in three straight games. Then we settled back to wait for the outcome of the Western finals between Minneapolis and St. Louis. When the Hawks won it, the stage was set for the playoff finals, a series which must rank with the most exciting set of basketball games ever played between two teams.

○

The excitement started in the very first game, which went to two overtime periods before we lost it 125 to 123. Sharman and I were hot in that game. Bill had 36 points and I had 26; so between the two of us we accounted for nearly half of the Celtics points. But it wasn't enough. Pettit with 37 was hotter than either of us. Jack Coleman settled it for St. Louis when he dunked in the clincher with seven seconds to go. I just missed one three seconds before the final gun in the second overtime, and I brooded about it for the rest of the night. All the points I piled up meant nothing because we'd lost the game.

We walked away with the second game, 119-99. Then on April 8 we played in St. Louis for the first time in the series. The fans there were the wildest I've ever seen, which didn't help us any. Tension was heightened when Red Auerbach punched Ben Kerner, the Hawks' owner, in an argument over the height of the basket, which Red wanted measured just before the game started. For this display of temper Red drew the astoundingly stiff fine of $300, which we all thought was grossly unfair. The fight also started rumors of feuds and grudges between the two teams which were completely un-unfounded. The whole series was cleanly played and well officiated.

The Hawks won the game 100-98—another thriller that was settled when Pettit sank a twenty-five-foot jump shot in the last seconds. But we evened the series at two games each before we left St. Louis by winning a fairly easy 123-118 decision in the fourth game. I had a big night with 31 points and so did Sharman with 24. Pettit was again the game's top man with 33 points.

We returned to Boston for the fifth game, which we won in a walk 124-109. Pettit had 33 points again, but he was the Hawks' only hot man. Sharman got 32, Heinsohn had 23 and I scored 21. Now we needed only one game to clinch the series, and we went back to St. Louis certain that we were going to end it—too certain, in fact. The Hawks didn't figure to have that good a team. Every game they played looked like their dying gasp.

I thought we were going to win that sixth game, despite

the fact that Pettit was still hot and Sharman and I were ice cold. At one time we had a six-point bulge, and we seemed to have fair control of the situation. But the Hawks refused to stay beaten. Jack McMahon caught fire and so did Cliff Hagan. Pettit had his usual terrific night, scoring 32 points. But McMahon and Hagan were killing us with key baskets. It was Hagan who finally finished us off.

The game was tied at 94-94, and with only a few seconds left, it looked like a certain overtime. But suddenly Pettit grabbed the ball and with a couple of seconds left shot one against the backboard. The ball never came down. Hagan was there to tip in the rebound and give the Hawks a 96-94 victory. That tied up the series and sent us all back to Boston for a Saturday afternoon winner-take-all final on April 13.

Once again we were confident. The Hawks surely figured to have played themselves out in that sixth game. They had to face us in the seventh with less than two days' rest, and they were playing us in our own backyard. The Boston Garden was sold out—a yelling, screaming mass of Celtics' fans, hungry for a championship they'd never known before.

But once again the Hawks refused to be beaten. They led us by two points at the end of the quarter and they still held a two-point advantage at the half. During the rest period before the second half began, nobody said much in our locker room. Red just told us to go out and play our game and class would tell. And when we led by six at the end of the third period, it looked as if that was just what would happen.

Sharman and I were still cold, but Heinsohn, Russell, Ramsey and Risen, particularly Heinsohn, were tremendous. The kid played his heart out, pouring in key baskets at times when we needed them most and using up every ounce of energy in that huge frame of his. But in spite of Heinsohn and the others, the Hawks made another dramatic comeback. They overcame the six-point deficit in the fourth period and actually went ahead at one point. Ramsey saved us with a key shot near the end that threw the game into overtime.

By this time, everyone in the place was hysterical. Bill and I were mad at ourselves for not helping more, but we stayed in there hoping we'd regain the touch we'd had in the earlier games. And Red stayed right with us. At no time did he toy with the idea of taking either of us out because we weren't hitting.

I messed up a chance to finish it without going into the second overtime. We were a point ahead with less than a minute to play when I got two foul shots. I moved up to the line, took my usual deep breath, bounced the ball a couple of times and quickly shot it in. That gave us a two-point lead. If I could sink my second foul, we'd be too far ahead for the Hawks to catch us in the few seconds remaining.

But Alex Hannum, the St. Louis coach, who, incidentally, did a magnificent job of keeping his team fired up, called a time out, and it gave me time to think. Under any circumstances it's not good to think too much about foul shots. They should be made more or less automatically. But I began figuring how to make that second shot. The first one had gone in but caromed off the backboard. I thought I ought to shoot the second one with a slightly softer touch, just to make sure it would hit.

So when time was back in, I stood at the foul line again. I looked at the basket, gauged the distance carefully, took my breaths, bounced the ball and then aimed it. I aimed too well. The shot was short. St. Louis got the ball and scored the tying points just before the buzzer.

We were tied again at the end of the first overtime, 113-113. Shortly after the second began Heinsohn fouled out and left the floor in tears. He was completely done physically and emotionally. He had played the game of his life, scoring 37 points and grabbing one rebound after another. He was so groggy that he started for the locker room, then turned and sat on the bench. Somebody gave him a towel, and he wrapped it around his face and buried his head between his knees. I don't know whether he saw the finish or not. All I know is that he gave everything he had, which was plenty, and kept us in the ball game.

We finally got the Hawks in that second overtime, but they didn't die easily. With seconds to go, we had a two-point lead. Hannum, who had to put himself in when all but four of his regulars had fouled out, had the ball deep in his own territory. He threw a desperation pass to Pettit, who had to turn for the shot. The ball hit the rim, rolled around one side of it and dropped out just as the buzzer went off.

I think I jumped ten feet. I forgot that miserable second foul miss, forgot that I'd sunk only two baskets from the floor in six periods, forgot the tension and the frustration and the constant pressure, forgot everything except that after seven long years I was finally part of a world's championship team. Everybody hugged everybody else as the delirious crowd swarmed down from the seats.

I don't know how I got back to the locker room, but finally I was there, smiling and happy in spite of my long afternoon of cold shooting. I was happy for Walter Brown, who had risked so much, and for Red Auerbach, who had taken so much, and for the fans and writers of Boston who had been so patient.

And I was happy for myself, too. I hadn't contributed much to this particular game, but I had satisfied my lifelong ambition.

I was with a winner at last.